World's Best Doctors

"Victoria is the very best friend and ally a physician can have during a time of crisis. She has helped me and many colleagues combat frivolous complaints over the years. There is nobody more skilled and capable! Through this book, she will share some of her 'secret sauce' for success in these matters. By the end, you will be more empowered to be a better physician. Her humor, competence, and down-home approach will serve all who read this to improve on their approach to all things clinical. Well done, Victoria!"

—*Allen W. Burton, MD, Houston, TX*

"Victoria Soto is more than an attorney—she is a leader. Victoria is highly sought after by health-care professionals throughout the nation. She sees the big picture and knows how to cast a vision and execute a plan for her clients and others. Victoria's book is a must-read for any physician."

—*Travis Lucas, senior partner, Lucas | Compton PLLC*

"The 'coarsening of American society' influences every sector of endeavor, including the medical profession. Victoria Soto has written a valuable tool to establish healthy physician and patient interactions—certainly a needed positive in today's culture as well as a means to reduce the risk of unnecessary litigation. This book should be a must-read for students and practitioners in the medical profession and beyond."

—*Major General Bob Dees, US Army, Retired;*
author, The Resilience Trilogy

"What a delightful and thought-provoking read. Victoria is a gifted genius, as is evidenced by her unique talent and ability for passionate engagement on behalf of her clients. As a friend, physician, and defense expert, who has worked with Victoria, I can personally attest to her charm, innate grasp of complex issues, and meticulous case preparation. As a result of her passionate engagement on behalf of her clients, she has an amazing and unmatched track record."

—*C. M. Schade, MD, PhD, PE*

"I'm honored to offer you my support with this book endeavor, Victoria. I'm also humbled at your work ethic in protecting physicians and all health-care professionals. You have such a caring passion for what you do that it puts your clients at ease. This alone is something not easily accomplished when you're dealing with surgeons!"

—Herve Gentile, MD, FACS

"Victoria Soto is one-of-a-kind. She is gentle, courteous, and pleasant to be around, yet persuasive and effective. She has a long record of successfully representing Texas physicians. Her engaging smile and personality light up a room. Victoria makes you want to help her obtain a just result for her client. Incorporating her suggestions into medical practice will help physicians help patients."

—Donald P. "Rocky" Wilcox, JD, Austin Attorney

"Victoria dissects out and brings to light the root of problems that can arise for physicians and advises how to recognize our flaws to prevent complaints and lawsuits. She offers advice from the perspective of a former prosecutor of physicians. If you have ever been accused of malpractice or subject to a board complaint or you want to be proactive and prevent one, then this book is for you. Victoria is faith based and exudes this in her writings, and her own words state it best: 'Truth and humility will prevail.' This book will help give you the same peace of mind she offers her clients."

—*John Ribeiro, MD, Texas*

"*World's Best Doctors* gives health-care providers a fresh way to look at applying a concept that is as old as the practice of medicine—having a good bedside manner. This book is enlightening, fun, and reflective at the same time. It shows the reader that having or cultivating a good bedside manner can go a long way in better patient care and satisfaction and can lead to a better relationship with fellow physicians and hospital staff, making for a more fulfilled and successful practice and career. It is a must-read for those wanting to work in medicine today."

—*Vernon F. Williams, MD, author*
of Grow Younger Like Me

"A passionate advocate for her clients, Victoria is truly one of a kind. While always their biggest supporter, she tactfully provides constructive criticism to even the most seasoned clientele, all in an effort to bolster their growth as professionals while representing them with masterful zeal.

With a heart as big as Texas (and a personality to match), she has crafted a modern-day "how-to manual" cradled in a book that is both entertaining to read and chock-full of useful information for those in the ever-changing medical profession. I would say it is a must-read, but I don't have to. You won't be able to put it down."

—*Mary Winston, JD, Austin, Texas;*
twenty years in practice, administrative law
attorney and member of the Texas Bar College

"*World's Best Doctors* provides relevant advice for health professionals through relatable scenarios. This book is perfect for students, early career professionals, and seasoned professionals."

—*DeAnna Harris-McKoy, PhD*

"I am so appreciative of Victoria Soto for this new work. We all often forget the power of courtesy and consideration and its profound impact on successful practices and business dealings. Thank you, Victoria, for reminding us of the basics. As a fellow attorney who works with clients to further their success from a legal perspective, it is noteworthy how many instances of legal trouble are rooted in a lack of consideration and inattentiveness to good manners. This book serves as a wonderful refresher on the importance of genuine courtesies and effective communication."

—*Lisa M. Tatum, LM Tatum, PLLC*

"I highly recommend reading *World's Best Doctors* for practical advice in lowering your risk of a complaint as well as improving patient and staff satisfaction. Written by a gifted attorney with massive experience in health-care law, the author worked early in her career as a prosecutor for the Texas Medical Board as well as for the majority of her career defending doctors from legal complaints.

I especially liked her storytelling style and the many examples of how a provider's communication and behavior with their patients and staff plays a great role in their risk of being sued. Why do many complaints get filed? Why should you be concerned about how they are defined? How should they be handled? How can you avoid complaints? The surprising truth is that bad manners are often a common cause of complaint.

A must-read for anyone currently practicing medicine. Buy the book *World's Best Doctors*, and become a better doctor."

—*Tom Diaz, MD*

WORLD'S BEST DOCTORS

WORLD'S BEST DOCTORS

How Good Old-Fashioned Manners

Improve Patient Satisfaction and Can Lower Litigation Risk

VICTORIA SOTO, JD

Published by Advantage, Charleston, South Carolina.
Member of Advantage Media Group.

ADVANTAGE is a registered trademark and the Advantage colophon is a trademark of Advantage Media Group, Inc.

Printed in the United States of America.

ISBN: 978-1-59932-632-0
LCCN: 2016939835

Book design by Matthew Morse

This publication is designed to provide accurate and authoritative information in regard to the subject matter covered. It is sold with the understanding that the publisher is not engaged in rendering legal, accounting, or other professional services. If legal advice or other expert assistance is required, the services of a competent professional person should be sought.

Advantage Media Group is proud to be a part of the Tree Neutral® program. Tree Neutral offsets the number of trees consumed in the production and printing of this book by taking proactive steps such as planting trees in direct proportion to the number of trees used to print books. To learn more about Tree Neutral, please visit **www.treeneutral.com.** To learn more about Advantage's commitment to being a responsible steward of the environment, please visit **www.advantagefamily.com/green**

Advantage Media Group is a publisher of business, self-improvement, and professional development books and online learning. We help entrepreneurs, business leaders, and professionals share their Stories, Passion, and Knowledge to help others Learn & Grow. Do you have a manuscript or book idea that you would like us to consider for publishing? Please visit **advantagefamily.com** or call **1.866.775.1696.**

Dedication

To my Lord God, for all that He is. To my mother, Mary Earline, an amazing woman and prayer warrior, who had faith in the doctors I have represented and prayed for their success in life. I dedicate this book to her; my amazing father, Lionel; my adoring husband, Jerry; my loving son, Cristian; and the rest of my wonderful family and friends. Many of these are the great and wonderful doctors I have had the honor and pleasure to work with for all these years. You are great healthcare providers and among the best doctors of the world, and I salute you.

Contents

Disclaimer

Throughout this book, you will find various fictitious stories of situations that could happen to physicians in this country—or any country, for that matter. They are written from years of legal experience in representing doctors and other healthcare professionals and are designed to give the reader a prospective of scenarios/parables in medicine and healthcare that could occur in any given situation to any licensed healthcare professional. Therefore, the scenarios/ parables found in this book, including but not limited to characters, names, businesses, places, events, and incidents are either the product of the author's imagination or used in a fictitious manner. Any resemblance to actual persons living or dead is purely coincidental. Although the author and publisher have made every effort to ensure that the information in this book was correct at press time, the author and publisher do not assume and hereby disclaim any liability to any party for any loss, damage, or disruption caused by errors or omissions. This book, *World's Best Doctors,* is designed to provide educational and authoritative information in regard to the subject matter covered, however, it is written and sold with the understanding that the author is not engaged in rendering specific, actionable legal advice. If you require legal advice or other expert assistance, you should seek the services of the author or another competent professional directly.

Introduction

I am writing this book for the amazing doctors, nurses, and healthcare providers of the world—the ones blessed with the gift to heal the heart, mind, and bodies of their patients, who have gone into the medical field for the right reasons, and who welcome opportunities to become better at everything they do.

I have met many doctors and nurses who have had nightmares about getting a complaint[1], getting sued for malpractice, and losing their licenses to practice. Because to them, losing their licenses means more than just the loss of their profession; it also means the loss of their life's work and how they define who they are. As a lawyer who has spent more than a decade working with, representing, and protecting doctors, I know that this is a very real concern.

---

1   For simplicity, "complaint" refers to a complaint or grievance before a licensing agency or a complaint or claim to an insurance company, a credentialing board, or the hospital, clinic, practice, or organization where you have privileges.

It is my intention that this book will help doctors and all healthcare providers to protect themselves against such threats to their work and to their sense of self.

On the other hand, there are also those healthcare providers and doctors who go about their days without a thought about such fears, and I am truly happy that they have that peace and grace about them. These doctors—who might not believe such a career-ending event could happen to them—may take this book as affirmation of their continued success, believing that they are an example of doctors who are doing things right and will continue to do so. But let me note that you do not need to be at fault to become the subject of a complaint regarding your license or the subject of a lawsuit. As I am sure you know, there need only be the *accusation* of fault. If such an event ever happens to you, you will need the skills and tools to survive such an assault on your career.

People may be surprised to discover that this book does not contain a lot of legal strategies. Instead, I want to talk about something that gets overlooked far too often in the medical profession—basic, good old-fashioned manners. A lot of doctors don't seem to realize that the difference between having a complaint filed against their licenses and *not* having one filed often has nothing to do with how well they've practiced their craft. Often, it is simply how they acted as human beings in a particular situation. The circumstances they find themselves in may simply come down to their manners, or the manners of others.

I am an attorney-at-law, so I can't teach you anything about how to perform surgery or become a better diagnostician. What I *can* offer you is the benefit of my experience on how you can interact with people in such a way that they may be less likely to file a formal complaint against you—whether you make a mistake in your practice or not. And there's evidence for this beyond what I know from my experience working with healthcare professionals in this world: Nalini Ambady, a social psychologist and researcher at Tufts University, showed that when people watched thirty-second clips of real physician-patient interactions, even with the sound off, they could judge a physician's "niceness"—and those judgments of the physician's niceness or lack thereof helped predict whether or not that physician would be sued. Her conclusion? When it came to things like lawsuits and complaints, physicians' personal manners were more important than their actual competence as doctors.[2]

But this is not the only benefit of good manners. The secret is that not only will good manners help to protect you from complaints, but they could also make you a better doctor, nurse, or healthcare provider. Plus, they could also make you a better person. And who wouldn't want that?

Who Am I?

I've been an attorney for more than twenty years. I was licensed and began practice in the state of Louisiana in 1995, then relocated to Texas in 1999. My professional focus for the entire time I've been in Texas has been in the healthcare arena, working with healthcare providers, agencies, and entities, mainly with a close and direct focus on doctors and other licensed healthcare professionals.

After moving to Texas, I began work as an investigator for the Texas State Board of Examiners of Psychologists. I went on to become the head of the enforcement division at this agency, enforcing disciplinary actions. This

---

2   Nalini Ambady et. al., "Surgeons' tone of voice: A clue to malpractice history," *Surgery* 132 (2002). http://web.stanford.edu/group/ipc/pubs/2002AmbadySurgery.pdf.

was the beginning of my experience with the healthcare world. Working in enforcement gave me a unique perspective on the different obstacles and issues that face healthcare providers and their interactions with patients and the families of patients. In 2001, I received my license to practice law in the state of Texas. The very day that I received my Texas State Bar Card, I walked across the lobby from the Psychology Board to the Texas Medical Board, where I applied to be a staff attorney. I was offered the job a few days later.

As a person of faith, I have always believed that it has been my calling to work in the medical community and to protect the licenses of doctors and other healthcare providers. You could say that the progression began with the job of understanding healthcare providers at the psychology board, then with prosecuting them as a staff attorney of the medical board, and finally defending the fine doctors and other healthcare professionals in front of their state agencies, hospitals, and health groups. Collectively, these positions have given me a very unique perspective on the practice of medicine, combining an understanding of doctors and how the world sees them with strategies to protect them in a world where they can be vulnerable to prosecution (and sometimes persecution). My close work with doctors in a nonmedical sense has given me an opportunity to see the heart and dedication that they have for their work.

The first thing I learned as an attorney in this field, and what you should understand as a physician licensed in any state, is that having a license to practice medicine is absolutely a *privilege*, not a right. Doctors sometimes get confused about that, and that's often when they start to have problems. As a prosecutor (staff attorney), I saw this come to light over and over again.

During my time at the medical board, I encountered cases where doctors had made mistakes in how they practiced medicine, of course, but after years of working on both sides from prosecutor to defense attorney, I noticed a prevailing trend. What I learned was that someone could be the best healthcare provider in the world—the best oncologist, neurologist, or plastics doctor in the country—but when it came to simple things like getting along with staffs, maintaining a professional relationship with competitors, interacting appropriately with patients and their families, or communicating well with others, he or she might fall short. It is my opinion that it was these shortcomings that more often than not prompted the complaints.

Even if a complaint actually stated that it was an issue of the standard of care or an issue of unprofessional conduct, after peeling away the layers, I would often find that the complaint stemmed from one of the causes mentioned above. A cause that may not have existed if proper manners had been applied.

Having had the privilege of working with doctors and healthcare providers these many years, I have typically found that the main reason a complaint is filed almost *always* has something to do with the healthcare provider's manners or behavior. In other words, the complaint against the doctors or health providers could generally be traced back to some flaw—not in how they practiced their craft but in how they acted toward people, whether it was their patients, a patient's family members, colleagues, or staff. A lack of good manners has been a problem in the practice of medicine that should not be ignored, and to do so is to the detriment of everyone in medicine.

As someone who has been involved both in prosecuting and defending healthcare providers, I believe that I have a well-rounded view of how the process works, which has served me very well in private practice. More importantly, I have been blessed to have worked with some of the very best doctors in the world, and this has given me the experience of seeing medicine practiced right and for the right reasons. I have seen what a difference that makes in the career of any doctor.

I do not profess to be the best person in the world to advise doctors. However, protecting the licenses of healthcare providers has been a great mission for me. I love what I do and feel blessed and honored to witness the success of a doctor freed from an investigation after his or her case is successfully resolved. I strive to be a peacemaker and mediator, always looking to find the solution that brings peace to both sides of a situation—so that the doctor can quickly find peace and focus his or her energy on helping patients and that the entity, agency, or court is satisfied that justice has been done and that the citizens and patients are protected.

My definition of success is getting the very best results possible for all parties involved. I was once told by a former executive of an agency where I defended a healthcare provider that when it came to the successful resolution of cases involving doctors, my numbers were significant and notable, and he wondered what was different about me. That was wonderful to hear. I thanked him, and credited my success in these cases to the amazing physicians, who were open to working through their cases with me and who had faith that at the end of the journey, truth and humility would prevail. It has truly been an honor to take that journey with them. I believe that success is a by-product of doing the right things for the right reasons.

I operate my practice as just a little one-mom shop, and my clients appreciate that when they hire me and get my personal attention as well as my many years of experience in this specific area. In doing this work, I have formed great relationships with some of the best expert physicians in the world. I have also had the privilege to work with wonderful professionals in the courts, agencies, and healthcare institutions that work with physicians. I understand how these entities work because of my interactions with them over many years. I also have a pretty good understanding of how important their work is, which is why I never see myself as working against any of them—even those who may be in a position to prosecute or investigate or review my client physicians. I see myself as working *with* them, and my hope is always that we have the same goal. At the end of the day, what I want most in any client's case is for good medicine to prevail and for the right thing to happen. Consequently, this means great patient care and a client who goes on to become a better practitioner because of it.

As the years have passed, I have come to realize that one of my greatest strengths is, for lack of a better word, "niceness." Actually, it's just simply part of who I am—but it's worked so well for me that I strongly advise others to try it. What's more, I believe it's a quality that can rub off on people in a "pay-it-forward" sort of way.

I've had clients who did not initially have the "niceness" trait but who later cultivated it and were happy that they did. Many have always been nice, and it made for a pleasant experience working with them. Still, others are clearly in sore need of the trait and will hopefully cultivate and acquire it with time. Most of us feel great comfort in the presence of a nice, kind, compassionate doctor—but those aren't qualities that are emphasized in medical schools or even in practice. But I truly believe these qualities *should* be greatly emphasized in medical schools and continued medical education.

I Wrote This Book for Doctors *and* Patients

One of the best strategies for protecting yourself as a doctor is to avoid getting a complaint or lawsuit in the first place. Of course, no one can entirely control the way other people react, but there are many ways that you, as a physician, can position yourself so that it's less likely that someone gets upset enough at you to want to cause you trouble. It is also incredibly important that healthcare providers position themselves to give the best medical care they can in the very best manner they can give. This can absolutely improve their relationships with their patients, which will improve overall patient care and satisfaction. This book will answer questions like:

- Why do many complaints/lawsuits get filed?
- Who may be filing these complaints and why?
- How are complaints defined, and why should you be concerned about them?
- How should you handle a complaint?
- What can you do to avoid complaints in the first place?

- Most importantly, how can you improve patient care and satisfaction?

It doesn't matter whether you're freshly out of medical school or a seasoned physician. It doesn't matter whether you are still learning or you are the best in the world in your field. I've had the privilege of working with individuals in all these categories and more. In my experience, everyone these days is in danger of being on the receiving end of a complaint or lawsuit.

You may not feel that you need this book, yourself, right now, but you may know someone who does. If this book can cause even a few doctors to change the way they work or behave for the better, or (if they've already had a complaint or lawsuit filed against them) to understand that the best way to survive the process is to modify any behavior that may have led to the situation, then I will feel like it's been successful.

The practice of medicine is, indeed, a noble and life-affirming profession. When people practice it well, when they practice it with kindness and empathy, they make a real impact on the lives of others—and, in kind, on the world. You never know whether or not the person you are treating or the life you just saved will change the world for the better. In your hands lies a great and immense responsibility that should never be taken lightly. I want to protect people like that. I want to help them protect themselves and be the best they can be so that they can go on to be of real service to others. I've seen healthcare providers successfully make the kinds of changes I talk about in this book, and it's had a real impact on both their professions and their lives.

At the end of the day, what I want for all my clients, and for everyone reading this, is peace of mind. I have often received letters and notes from clients that have moved me and reminded me of my purpose and mission in life, which, once again, is to protect doctors and other healthcare providers so that they may learn from their experiences and get on with the business of delivering babies, curing illness, alleviating pain, and so on.

Here is an example of an especially moving letter that has inspired me for years:

Dear Victoria,

Thank you. In thinking about what my family and I have been through since the beginning of this complaint, it is clear to me that it was not only the facts of the case but how you prepared me and showed your faith in me and my work that I believe was responsible for getting the resolution that allowed me to get back to the practice of medicine. You and your wonderful staff were able to get me to focus as I pulled myself together and remembered who I was as a human being and as a physician. It was amazing how you prepared me to face the facts of the case and the judging forum. It was in the spirit of truth and honesty. Your stressing this made me feel confident to walk into what would have normally been a scary situation. For me, the most important part of the preparation was that you calmed my concerns and any fears I might have had. You did this by allowing me to focus on the truth of my practice and treatment of my patients.

As a professional in the healthcare field, I'm sure you can relate to how gratifying it is to receive the sincere thanks of someone whose life you've impacted. I wrote this book in the hope that through my experiences and storytelling, you will be able to focus more on those individuals who have thanked you for your great treatment and less on worrying about what happens if someone files a complaint.

At the end of the day, the relationships you cultivate both as a professional and as a human being truly matter. And you can start making a difference by improving in any of these simple interactions:

- how you say good morning to the custodian as you enter the hospital
- how you interact with the nurses or techs who assist you
- how you say please when you need something
- how you say thank you when you get it
- how you sincerely ask the patient how he or she is doing

Each interaction makes a difference in the short term but also five or ten years later, when you run into patients from years ago who still remember the way you made them feel respected at such an important time in their lives, or when you meet a mother and the baby you delivered—now an adult and running for city council. On another note, you may find yourself in need of a letter stating that you're a good man or woman, despite what a complaint filed against you says. In such an instance, colleagues who remember what a good and giving person you are can write testimonial letters on your behalf. It all boils down to a simple fact of life: *how you behave today can absolutely affect your tomorrow.*

CHAPTER 1:

Why You Need Good Manners

*What kinds of cases could possibly have to do
with having better manners? Read on:*

Dr. Make-Me-Beautiful walked into her office. As usual, the office glistened with its clean walls and works of art on display. She wanted it to look like a beautiful contemporary museum with warm tones and clean lines—a place to admire all kinds of art, including her work in plastic surgery. It was beautiful and the patients did love it. For that reason alone, the doctor was pleased. This particular morning appeared to be a beautiful one. The doctor had a light schedule of only two lipos and one tuck to review and do pre-op. What the good doctor did not expect to find on her pristine desk was a crisp, white envelope from her medical board. Inside the envelope, she found a notice of a complaint, which stated that she had allegedly violated the medical board rules and regulations regarding her patient. Upon review of this letter and the patient's name, she was very confused. She knew with certainty she had performed a flawless procedure for this patient and even recalled the patient being very pleased with the outcome.

What in the world brought this on? Dr. Make-Me-Beautiful moved from the quietness of her office and went into the outer office and whispered to the receptionist to send in the office manager, who soon appeared with a knowing, concerned look on her face. The office manager had, of course, been the individual who put the envelope on the doctor's desk and had been waiting for this moment. The doctor handed her the envelope and asked if she had any idea what brought this on. Apparently, the office manager said, the patient was not satisfied with the balance of her bill and had called up about a week prior and argued with the billing department. The patient had been fully informed about the cost associated with her procedure, so the bill should not have come as a surprise to her. However, because of that argument between the billing manager and the patient, this doctor was now accused of violating rules. Not rules associated with billing—but with the way the doctor and her staff had treated the patient. The money issue and her not wanting to pay her bill was conveniently left out of the complaint that was made to the Board.

As her attorney's law office conducted its own investigation of this complaint as the Board's formal investigation progressed, Dr. Make-Me-Beautiful was informed that her billing manager had used abrasive language and behavior toward not only the patient at issue but several other patients, who had questions about the fees. It was one thing to have a strict policy about the paying of fees in one's office but another to encourage bullying patients unkowingly, by her bullying nature and mannerisms, into paying their outstanding balance.

Later, during the Board's investigation and litigation process, Dr. Make-Me-Beautiful was informed that staff had testified in sworn affidavits that it was her no-tolerance policy that made them feel compelled to lean on the patients for payment and that her employees were afraid of the consequences if this type of pressure was not enforced. The doctor was astounded to hear her supervising skills being described this way. When, in preparing for the defense of her license, it was revealed that the majority of her staff were genuinely afraid of her, she had to take a long, hard look at her behavior from a spectator's point of view.

The description of her walking into her office earlier in this story read as though it was a beautiful, picturesque environment. One where you could almost hear the music of Vivaldi playing in the background and the clouds opening up through the windows to show a clear blue sky, as she glided through her waiting room as though she were an angel floating was a vision belonging solely to the doctor. The reality was much different from her staff and patients' perspectives. When Dr. Make-Me-Beautiful walked into her office, everyone went silent out of fear. The receptionists whispered that the witch was headed down the hall. The doctor did not acknowledge her staff at the lobby desk, though they tried to get her attention. The patients in the waiting room tried to greet her, but she did not acknowledge them, as though they were objects to be moved about on her playing board. She perceived this as acceptable behavior. She even saw her "light" schedule—two lipos and one tuck—as procedures and not patients who entrusted their lives to her.

Beneath her chronic bad behavior, she was a fabulous, precise, brilliant plastic surgeon. However, her manners were so awful that it left her vulnerable for a catastrophic career event. Had she not pressured her staff to behave badly and work in a place of fear and had she not treated her patients as though they were procedures instead of human beings, she very well may have avoided the complaint.

In the end, Dr. Make-Me-Beautiful had to admit the truth to herself and learn from it and take responsibility. She improved her behavior so that people could begin to respond to her positively and not in fear. She ultimately learned that to those around her, having good manners actually created a true and real environment of friendliness and kindness that showed true beauty in her office and resulted in a healthier workplace and place of healing for her patients.

Dr. Watercooler

Suppose you are a doctor who has *great* relationships with your patients—but then a complaint comes in from a source you never would have expected. This happened to Dr. Watercooler.

Dr. Watercooler walked into his home after a long shift at the hospital. The ER had been a madhouse. Those full-moon nights never fail to produce a bevy of strange traumas. On the cool granite top of his kitchen bar he finds a stack of mail, and as he thumbs through it, he sees a letter addressed to him from the hospital review board, informing him that human resources had received a complaint regarding his unprofessional conduct. He was floored—he could not imagine where this could have come from! Dr. Watercooler had a great relationship with everyone at the hospital. He had worked there for more than thirty years, and he treated everyone like family. His patients loved him, so it could not be as a result of a patient complaint.

HR reviewed the complaint, and unfortunately, it found its way to a review and investigation by the doctor's licensing agency. As the process continued, Dr. Watercooler did some soul searching and had to admit that sometimes, while on call and in the staff lounge or rotation desk, he had a habit of chatting about personal issues and engaging in seemingly innocent chatter about popular television dramas that aired the night before. Often, without realizing it, he would become so involved with his casual conversation that he didn't realize that others were within earshot who did not appreciate such talk in the workplace. Patients and staff found it incredibly distracting and unprofessional. It turned out that on more than a few occasions, his comments about a racy plot on a TV show were taken out of context and reported as if he were using inappropriate language toward hospital staff. Though all of this appeared to have little or nothing to do with the practice of medicine, Dr. Watercooler still found himself on the receiving end of a complaint. And regardless, this type of behavior could hurt even a well-established doctor like Dr. Watercooler. In any case, it tarnished his whole reputation in the eyes of the complainant, who turned out to be a well-trained nurse. Given enough time, the perfect storm of events and circumstances between Dr. Watercooler and this nurse could escalate, and a more medically driven complaint could very well come next—simply because the nurse was offended by Dr. Watercooler's television talk. What someone may think or feel can be crucial to whether or not he or she files a complaint. It's often sad for doctors to find out that what started out as a personality conflict or wrong perception snowballed into a whopper of a complaint.

These scenarios happen all the time in real life, and, as I said in the opening of this book, many doctors have nightmares about them—or at least they should. There's a lot at risk for physicians and other healthcare professionals and the places they work. All of the time, effort, and cost spent in training and building a private practice or association with a hospital could be taken away by their licensing agency as a result of a career-damaging claim or suit. Medical boards have the power to grant you a license to practice medicine, and they certainly have the power to revoke that privilege—for as little as one complaint. Many times, revocations come on the heels of comprehensive complaints that send a career down in flames. These may have been sparked by a tiny ember many years before, even prior to medical school. Let me explain:

Dr. Luca-To-Futura:

Dr. Luca-To-Futura is handsome and determined. His father was a successful orthopedic surgeon for twenty years. His brother is a successful pediatrician. Dr. Luca-To-Futura started medical school because he was determined to follow in his family's footsteps and become a successful neurosurgeon. Unfortunately, his first year was a rough one because he could not take the pressure of measuring up to his father and brother and his fear of failing. He had a few issues with the campus police due to partying excessively and fighting with a girlfriend. He also had a great sense of entitlement because of his father's reputation and position in the small community, and this led to disrespectful behavior, such as cutting lectures and dismissing the imposed requirements of the probation.

Dr. Luca-To-Futura drastically changed his perspective over the summer and returned to school determined to straighten up his act—and indeed, he quickly became a model student. Unfortunately, after graduation and upon his entry into residency, his old demons began to resurface. As an actual doctor, his arrogance grew and so did his reputation for it. Upon completing his residency, Dr. Luca-To-Futura applied for a medical license, and the medical boards asked him to answer questions regarding any disciplinary action that he had experienced in medical school and residency, etc.

He had been counseled in medical school and by his residency program director that the actions taken against him in medical school or residency, such as his academic probation or program probation, were considered issues that were *not* reportable. This is not necessarily true. In most cases, the medical school would not report it to the school or another entity, so it would *normally* not be held against the student or young doctor. But, when a medical board requests information, often the school will hand the information over without another thought. Unfortunately, this occurred in Dr. Luca-To-Futura's situation and it was a very serious mistake on his part. Upon request, his medical school and residency program gave everything it had to the requesting board—including his academic probation and his school behavior record. In the end, in order to defend himself, he had to explain why the fact that he was on probation was not something he believed should be disclosed to the licensing agency. Dr. Luca-To-Futura did not believe that he was being deceptive and believed that the issues he had gone through were, in fact, not reportable, even by him.

Dr. Luca-To-Futura was defenseless against the facts presented because he could not change the past, and his excuse that he did not believe it to be reportable is generally not accepted. It may be understood but not accepted, and the licensing board could see it as deceptive. If you have to ask yourself whether an issue is reportable to the asking entity and you're not sure, please ask someone who should know before you enter the wrong answer for what you believe to be the right reason. Telling the truth is always the best way, and in this situation, Dr. Luca-To-Futura did not. Also, when asked if he could provide letters of recommendation from colleagues in residency to attest to his improved behavior, he could find very few. His attitude of superiority and arrogance had isolated him from his fellow residents, and all he could do in response was display his many awards for his research and other clinical success in residency—and, when asked by someone assisting him in getting ready to respond why he did not receive any letters of recommendation, his response was to say that his colleagues were all jealous of his brilliance. Unfortunately, having good manners and treating others as you would want to be treated was a lesson that escaped him.

There is no telling how far back Dr. Luca-To-Futura had to reflect to get to the root of his behavioral issue, but he eventually got there. He faced the grim reality of what his behavior nearly cost him, and then realized (finally) that having proper manners and respect for others can be a valuable thing. Dr. Luca-To-Futura is brilliant and will go on to do great things in the field of medicine and science, but his short-sighted behavior nearly derailed his future. His story is a great cautionary lesson to both young and seasoned doctors.

Dr. Luca-To-Futura aside, the role of licensing agencies, credentialing agencies, hospitals, and the courts is all too real to a doctor's future. These organizations focus on what's safest for the patient, so even a seemingly unwarranted complaint may be a long, arduous process to resolve. Past behavior can come back to haunt you when you need a character recommendation to attest to your talents. Complaints like these can take a year or more and feel like an anvil hanging over your head, even if you're certain you've done nothing wrong. What's more, complaints can have a way of sticking to you and doing real damage to your reputation, even if you are cleared of the charges in the end.

To give yourself a better chance of avoiding complaints like these, the best defense is to avoid receiving them in the first place—and while that's not entirely within your power, there is a lot you can do to get the odds on your side. I offer this perspective not just so you can avoid the bad things that could result from a complaint but also so you can go forth and practice medicine in the best possible circumstances. As you go about your day, helping people to live pain-free or curing children of diseases or making wonderful and lifesaving breakthroughs in the world of medicine, the last thing you want on your mind is a state agency and/or hospital weighing whether or not to take disciplinary action against you. You want a clear conscience and focus, which is exactly what I want for you and for all my clients.

If Dr. Make-Me-Beautiful, Dr. Watercooler, and Dr. Luca-To-Futura are not proof enough to really examine your actions and what you can do to avoid getting complaints in the first place, then read on.

Complaints to Any Healthcare or Licensing Entity Could End Your Career

One of the reasons you should take the potential for complaints seriously is that when caps are put on how much a patient can sue a doctor for, then complaints to a physician's hospital board or licensing agency often rise as a result. There are some who decide that if they cannot get the message out via a traditional medical malpractice lawsuit, then perhaps the best solution for receiving satisfaction might be to file a complaint with the licensing agency. The chances on a settlement of a suit may rise if there has been some action taken against that doctor by his or her license agency or hospital. If the licensing agency or hospital decides there has been some wrongdoing, then the chance of a successful lawsuit or an insurance settlement could be more likely.

The change in laws in many states regarding caps on how much a doctor can be sued for has been a double-edged sword for doctors. Many doctors thought to themselves, *Oh wow, a cap on lawsuits—that is wonderful!* What they didn't realize was that a disciplinary action from a licensing agency or a disciplinary action from a hospital where they had privileges could be far more grueling and damaging than a lawsuit.

The way medicine is practiced has changed in recent years as a result of the Affordable Care Act[3] and rising healthcare costs. Doctors, reportedly, are increasingly under pressure to see more patients in a shorter amount of time while giving the same quality of care. I have been told too often by many of them that they are discouraged from spending more than ten to fifteen minutes per patient because it is not cost effective. This cautionary message comes from whatever practice they are a part of or the entity responsible for paying for the treatment of their patients. Ten to fifteen minutes is not a lot of time, and it certainly would not go far in giving patients confidence in their treatment. Patients, in this scenario, could easily feel as though they are products on a conveyor belt, rather than human beings

---

3   You can find more information on the Affordable Care Act at www.health-care.gov.

in need of care and compassion. When patients are left to feel this way, things can become explosive. This can very well lead to more complaints — both because patient care goes down when there isn't enough time to communicate and because patients feel less satisfied by the experience. Most people don't want their doctor to treat them like just another number or to be defined by their procedure, as we saw in the case of Dr. Make-Me-Beautiful.

What's even worse is that those doctors who try to go against the grain and say, "No, I'm going to spend twenty or thirty minutes—not ten—talking to this patient because that's what he or she needs," can be setting themselves up for a complaint from a different source. In recent years, there has been a rise in complaints filed against doctors believed to be fueled by big corporations or those that believe that doctors should get with the program of "big money" which to some, translates into taking the focus off of "good medicine." These complaints also come from fellow health-care providers who are not independent enough to refuse to take part in a "get-rid-of-a-doctor-who-won't-get-with-the program" scheme.

I know all of this can sound scary, but there are physicians who have experienced it. On the other hand, there are those who may read this and feel far removed from the possibility and see this book as a series of sensationalized stories. My hope for those who *are* experiencing it is that you survive it—and for those who are oblivious, that you remain so, live long, and prosper.

Call me an idealist, but I still believe in the good of humanity and that there are good people at the helm of these big businesses who are actually fighting for good patient care. Thank you, you Good Samaritans of health-care. Continue to fight for what is good—such as doctors taking the time they need with their patients. Fight against those that cause the quality of healthcare to go down for the sake of money. Turn that big corporation around and use it for the sake of good healthcare.

Fighting the Good Fight: Dr. Goodbody

An orthopedic surgeon recently worked with a patient who survived being crushed by a tractor-trailer truck and began receiving worker's compensation. Dr. Goodbody received a letter from the patient's insurance company stating that they were not going to cover the treatment because, according to the medical reviewer, the patient's treatment was "no longer indicated". This was very frustrating and incredible for Dr. Goodbody who believed that he was being pressured by the payor company to stop treating this patient. The payor attached a letter from a medical reviewer stating that the treatment rendered was no longer indicated and this patient was good to return to work. This letter was signed by a medical reviewer even though Dr. Goodbody's evaluation, diagnostic tests and medical notes all showed that this patient clearly had not recovered and was unable to return to work.

"Absolutely not. I'm not going to stop treating this person," Dr. Goodbody said. "This is a human being who is in real pain, and the medical records clearly show what this patient is going through."

In response, such payor companies may file a complaint against the doctor, who is just sticking up for his or her patient, and it becomes an ugly situation.

The good thing is that even though complaints like these are rising, medical boards, and all other healthcare entities and agencies are made up of human beings who are good people, and once these good people see that a complaint is groundless, they often dismiss it. They do not want to hurt a good physician, because to hurt a good physician is to hurt his patients and his future patients. It is my hope, belief, and faith that no one wants to keep a good doctor from doing what he or she is best at.

Because Complaints Can Come from Anywhere

Doctors who are lucky enough never to have had a complaint filed against them tend to not worry at all, or worry most about the potential for a complaint coming from one of their patients. That's a legitimate concern, but it surprises some people to learn that complaints can really come from anywhere.

As I mentioned before, "big business" sometimes files complaints. Complaints can also come from your competitors, like the doctor across town who hears about or sees your great work and is envious of your success or disagrees with how you treat patients. They can also come from the people who currently work in your office and from people who have worked for you in the past—like a doctor you hired to help with your practice, a nurse, assistant, or receptionist.

Complaints can also come from the people who work with you in one of the hospitals where you have privileges, even if they aren't working with you directly most of the time. Believe it or not, these complaints can come from any of the healthcare workers in these hospitals that you encounter—including but not limited to technicians, custodians, lunchroom staff, and of course, nursing staff and fellow doctors. That may astound you. However, it has happened through these sources, and since many times the identity of the complainant is anonymous, you would not know. Or, it could be an ex-employer filing a complaint, irritated that you have more talent than he or she has or that you've moved on to another practice without giving much notice of your departure. Or it could be a hospital administrator trying to get rid of you to make room for new, less costly staff in your position.

Sometimes it's even someone from your personal life who files a complaint, like a disgruntled wife, husband, girlfriend, or boyfriend. That person may bring up all the things you mentioned in pillow talk that you should have kept to yourself or the times you prescribed medication to them or various family members without keeping a record of it (which is not good, by the way). Whether you actually did what they reported or not, it can still wreak havoc on your life.

And, of course, it could be a patient who is unhappy with his or her treatment—or a patient who is unhappy with how you treated him or her personally, even though your medical treatment for their condition was more than above the standard of care. It could be your treatment *of them* not *for them* that matters.

The point is that *anyone* you come into contact with can potentially file a complaint against you. That is worth thinking about because—in case you didn't already realize it—your professionalism and your behavior is always being judged by others. That's why I hope this book encourages you to take a broad view of not just your bedside manner when treating patients but also your manner toward people in general.

Because Complaints Can Become Public: Dr. Net-Forever

Dr. Net-Forever, on his way to the airport for a conference, stops at a red light and, as is his bad habit, pulls out his smartphone to check his text messages, and on the newsreel bar of his phone pops up his favorite new site, "BadDoc-Watch.com." (Any similarity to an actual site is purely coincidental and, I am sure, inevitable.) He can't help himself;

he is obsessed with this site, all the while knowing that he would never be on it (and hoping secretly that his competitor across town *would* be on it). Suddenly, a horn blows to alert him to drive on. However, he is stuck in place as the cars drive around him—because the name he sees being blasted across the screen is his own. A patient has decided to blog about the treatment his mother received in Dr. Net Forever's office.

Later, after reviewing the chart, Dr. Net-Forever saw that the care was appropriate and that there was a good outcome with the patient. However, what was not on the chart was the perceived slight that the patient's son felt when the doctor appeared to refuse to answer a question about his mother's care—when the doctor gave him, what he thought was an oversimplified answer. Dr. Net-Forever mistakenly judged this man's knowledge base, due to his disheveled attire that day. The son was furious and decided that he would let the world know what a jerk Dr. Net-Forever was. This incident also resulted in a complaint to the health authority and licensing agency. Dr. Net-Forever is still fighting to get his name removed from the site and working through the various complaints filed.

Dr. Net-Forever's scenario, unfortunately, happens frequently and is a big reason why doctors want to avoid complaints and poor patient care; not only is poor patient care a sign that they are not perfect doctors, but complaints can quickly go public. We're living in the time of the Internet, and, fair or not, once something is out there, it's out there in perpetuity.

When a complaint is lodged with a doctor's licensing agency at a state level, an investigation regarding a complaint against his or her license can be resolved at an informal conference and can result in disciplinary action or dismissal. However, if not resolved by an agreed-upon disciplinary action between the doctor and the licensing agency, a formal complaint may be filed (depending on the state), and then it may head to a trial. An administrative complaint by a licensing agency may be resolved by an administrative court finding and/or recommendation. In a civil proceeding, it may also be resolved by settlement, before or after trial. In both situations, administrative and civil, any resolution that is not dismissed will be made public—on the doctor's record and floating in the cloud in Internet space forever. A disciplinary action against a doctor is usually also reported to the National Practitioner

Data Bank (NPDB), which any hospital or health institute has access to, and this could affect future hiring or hospital privileges.

The thing to understand is that the information that gets released to the public may not be the end of the story. Once the disciplinary action's time has expired and all components are satisfied, it may eventually be gone from the physician's record, but, as stated above, it is still out there on the Internet forever, to be asked about and explained. It is a gift that could keep on giving—in a way the doctor wishes it wouldn't.

With or without a formal complaint, patients are increasingly using informal sources online to find out what sort of reviews are out there about the physicians they are considering, even though the information is not always accurate. There are review sites specifically geared toward doctors, where anyone can air grievances in an informal way, with few checks and balances. I've had doctors tell me that minor complaints and even complaints that were dismissed entirely but circulated on these review sites have severely damaged their careers.

This just shows how high the stakes can be. It's heartbreaking when a physician's reputation is damaged for something he or she didn't do or for something that is a relatively small offense like a record-keeping violation. But that's the world we live in, and there's no use pretending any differently. That's one of the big reasons why, if at all possible, you want to avoid having a complaint filed against you in the first place.

On the Record: Dr. Unfortunate-Bystander

Take the case of Dr. Unfortunate-Bystander, who received a complaint that she was the cause of grave harm to a patient she'd treated in the hospital. The complaint was devastating, even though there was absolutely no evidence of the doctor being the cause of any harm to the patient. In fact, she'd actually initiated lifesaving efforts to save the patient when other treatment-center personnel, including the patient's regular doctor, didn't respond.

Dr. Unfortunate-Bystander's case went through the entire investigation phase. When the patient's full record was seen by the reviewing agency, they said, "Now that we've seen all of the medical records, we think you're a very good doctor. You did everything correctly in your treatment of this patient." However, it was also noted that the doctor would not have been to the point of a face-to-face review (hearing) in the first place if she had remembered to make one particular notation in this case. Many times, not having the time, or some may say not having the good manners, to complete the medical record can compromise patient care and put the physician at risk of receiving disciplinary action. Just think of it, if it is not written, then there is no evidence that it occurred. Examples of what physician notes or records could prove are as follows: that "the patient was counseled as to the risk of this procedure", or "the physician discussed the procedure with the patient prior to the surgery", or "the physician discussed the case with the doctor on call prior to leaving for the evening". If not for a flawed—even ever so slightly—medical record, the case of Dr. Unfortunate-Bystander might have been dismissed very early on. As a result of an incomplete medical record, a reviewing agency required the doctor to undergo continuing medical education (CME).

In this scenario, the source of the complaint is filed by hospital staff. In getting Dr. Unfortunate-Bystander ready for her hearing, her legal team found out that she had a bad habit of speaking down to staff, whom she considered to be less educated and "not on her level". The doctor didn't even realize this bad habit. After this "less than desired" manner of feeling superior was uncovered, she had to forgive herself and realize that it could have very well been the reason that her impeccable career could be negatively affected. By improving how she spoke and interacted with others, she would fare much better in the world, and it would be less likely that people would want to damage her career.

As stated earlier in the book, it's important to note that patients don't get any money from filing a complaint against a doctor with the doctor's medical board or agency, but they can get a feeling of justice. The filing of a complaint could, however, fuel a civil action or claim down the line, or the latter could trigger the former. If the complaint is successful, the agency, hospital, or credentialing board can revoke a physician's license, privileges, or position if the circumstances require such action. Then the patient can say to him or herself that the doctor may have wronged me, but at least he won't be able to harm another person, and he will pay for the wrong he did in some form of suffering or compensation.

I will be the first to say that if there is bad medicine or a bad doctor involved, then that doctor's wrongdoing should be addressed effectively. This is necessary for good patient care, and it is a sentiment that all good doctors share.

When a good doctor is at fault, trust me, no one wants a proper resolution or investigation to take place more than the doctor. Good doctors understand that good medicine benefits from discovering the origins of mistakes. This is not a criminal justice venue, but there are occasions when the criminal justice system will step in.

The majority of complaints that we actually see in this country are not about bad doctors doing bad things. Doctors are not perfect, of course, and they can make mistakes, but the vast majority of them are good people trying their best to help others. We live in a country where we have access to some of the best physicians in the world. They're highly trained and innovative, on the cutting edge of medicine. They're compassionate about their patients, and very passionate about what they do. That's exactly the kind of doctors I've had the privilege to work with over the course of my career. They're all good people at heart, but sometimes they make poor decisions, and sometimes bad things are seemingly done to them for no good reason— apart from a lack of manners, which can be remedied.

I've represented doctors who have practiced for two years, five years, fifty years, and beyond. Most clients come to me after receiving a complaint for the first time in their career, sometimes after having practiced longer than I have been alive. Every doctor has the potential of being in the kinds of situations that this book describes, whether they are new to the job or well seasoned—even if they are the absolute best in their field.

Most young people studying to become doctors don't realize that whenever they attempt to get a license in a new state, the scrutiny of their behavior will start with their records from medical school. That means that from the very beginning of your career, it is important to understand what sort of behavior or manner can lead to some sort of disciplinary action and what sort of behavior or manner will simply make you better at what you do.

You should use the skill of good manners—being kind and respectful to those around you—as a tool from the beginning of your career, all the way through to your retirement. Manners always matter, no matter who you are, what you do, or where you are in your career. If having good manners can help you avoid complaints and avoid your being brought before your licensing agency or hospital review board then obviously you will benefit, as will everyone in your presence as you practice medicine and go through life. But that's not the end of the story.

If you take this advice to heart, you may find that you will end up treating people better—not just medically but also in a way that they feel cared for and listened to. Once again, this can make you not only a better doctor but also a better human being, and that can impact a great deal of people—basically anyone you work with or associate with and most importantly, your patient.

CHAPTER 2:

What Are Good Manners?

Plain, old-fashioned good manners may be something of a lost art in the medical field, but that doesn't make them unimportant. Of course, for many people, good manners are simply part of life, but some doctors tell me that it's the one thing they aren't taught in medical school, which is really a shame. Manners should be a required course for every physician.

Because manners aren't something most doctors learn in medical school, they have to learn through experience, which could mean being mentored by supervisors early in their careers and watching other doctors in action. Of course, the obvious way doctors *should* have learned good manners is through their parents. But sometimes it sticks, sometimes it is forgotten, and sometimes it is just not taught in the home environment. Unfortunately, the development of good behavior and manners too often comes through pain; it is often only when a complaint is filed against them that doctors who haven't learned these all-important lessons find that what they thought were normal and acceptable behaviors aren't appreciated in a hospital or clinical setting.

The question that may be coming to your mind as you read this is what exactly do I mean when I use the term "good manners"? That's what this chapter is about. It will give you a clearer understanding of the kinds of behaviors that I believe—based on many years of experience working with and defending doctors—every physician should be practicing when dealing with people. And it will include some behaviors that you may not have even considered.

Why does all this matter? I'll get more into that as well, but for now I'll say that I have spoken to many physicians who said, "I was not the only doctor involved in the care and treatment of this patient. There were four doctors involved, so why is it that I am the one who received the complaint?" The reason almost always has to do with the fact that the other three doctors had better relationships with the source of the complaint. Better manners foster better relationships.

One would think the complained-against doctor in such a situation was probably the main doctor handling the patient's care—but that is not always so. I have had several cases where that wasn't the case. What my clients and I would often find as we worked backward, peeling back the layers of what happened, was that had it not been for their callous treatment of the family during a difficult circumstance, they probably would not have had a complaint filed against them either. However, to the family who filed the complaint, my client's behavior came across as arrogant, whereas the main doctor on the case was well liked and sympathetic toward them. It all really came down to that one difference in the doctors' manners.

When I talk about displaying good manners as a doctor, I'm really talking about being a good human being. I mean someone who truly cares about patients and patient outcomes. I mean someone who cares about the patient's family and shows sympathy and understanding when communicating with them. I mean someone who is honest and has integrity. I mean someone who treats all people with respect. These are qualities that the best physicians possess. Even if, on the surface, highly successful and gifted doctors come across as having a strong ego, they absolutely *can* be kind and giving and great humanitarians at the same time. These are not things that get in the way of success; they are things that help you attain it.

Having proper manners starts with good old-fashioned common sense. Unfortunately, it's sad to see how rare common sense actually is in some cases. Good manners start with being true to self and having self-respect. That may sound like a selfish thing, but it's not. It's like being on the airplane and the stewardess says, "Please put the oxygen mask on yourself before proceeding to help the person next to you." It's about being as whole and as healthy as you can be so that you have something to give to other people.

Having respect for yourself allows you to have respect for others. When I say that, I mean having respect in the deepest possible way so that others can truly feel it. You can't just provide care for your patients; it has to come across that you *genuinely care* about them. It has to come across that you care about what happens not only to them as patients but as fellow human beings. Patients want to see and feel this type of respect in their doctor before they allow themselves to be treated. Let's be honest—who wants someone who does not show basic respect and empathy to examine them or cut into them on the operating table? Would you want a person like that as your doctor?

When you actively care about someone, it's not just something that happens in your head. It's about how you act. It's about helping someone feel comfortable telling you what's wrong with him or her. You have to make eye contact, use a friendly and approachable tone of voice, pick up on reactions to what you're saying and doing, and listen and respond thoughtfully to what's being said. A very key thing to being a good physician is *observation*. You have to be able to observe all sorts of things about your patient so that you know what questions to ask, how to interact with them, and ultimately, how to treat them for what ails them. But if you're so self-involved that you cannot take the time to look up from your chart or listen to what the patient is saying, then you could miss out on a whole lot, both medically and personally. And that could be a potential problem for your patient.

From this point, it is about having the mindset that you can be of service. To truly be of service, you have to be the best that you can be at your job. You have to understand what makes people hurt, what makes them happy, what makes them healthy, and what makes them unhealthy. And you have to understand that having good manners makes people feel better and more willing to open up to you, more willing to trust you.

When choosing a doctor, aside from the obvious choice of whether a doctor has the qualifications and experience to render the treatment needed, patients look for someone who:

- has common sense
- has self-respect
- has reverence and respect for others
- is actively kind and caring, so others can feel it
- wants to be of service to others

Bedside Manner vs. All-around Good Manners

The qualities of the world's best doctors don't just apply to your interactions with patients. Qualities like being respectful and caring and wanting to be of service to others should come into play with *anyone* you interact with. Being observant and aware of the effect you're having will enhance the quality of your relationships beyond just the doctor-patient relationship. These are the same qualities that make you a good colleague in the hospital or office setting, a good boss of your office staff, and a good mate to whomever you share your life with. They are the same qualities that you want to have no matter what the relationship is.

Bedside manner is a term often used when talking about physicians, and it's defined as: "A popular term for the degree of compassion, courtesy, and sympathy displayed by a physician toward patients in a clinical setting" (*Concise Dictionary of Modern Medicine*, s.v. "Bedside Manner"). That's a good definition, but I believe physicians really need to think about their manners in terms that are broader than that. This definition is limited in the sense that it refers only to the doctor's relationship with his or her patients. What I'm talking about here applies to the patient relationship, certainly, but also to how the doctor interacts with *everyone else*. This is about the degree of compassion, courtesy, sympathy, and professionalism that a doctor displays when interacting with anyone—patients, colleagues, mid levels, nursing staff, administrators, hospital techs and office tech staff, receptionists, custodians, lunchroom workers, and people on the street. I mean literally *everyone*.

That's because, as I noted in the last chapter, a complaint can come from anyone, not just a patient. Again, the majority of complaints I've seen don't have to do with the prescription you wrote or how well you wield a scalpel. They're usually not about the symptoms you missed, your misdiagnosis, or a mistake you made during surgery. Sure, the complaint or grievance will probably have a standard-of-care bullet in it—and sometimes bad medicine does, in fact, happen—but once you peel back the onion of the case, you will often find that the origin or seed of the complaint was more about your personal behavior toward someone you came into contact with while practicing medicine.

This is the reason why many complaints don't actually get past the first stage of an investigation. With some health agencies and with some hospital systems, in general, a complaint to your superiors may never even come across your radar because its root may be uncovered as not having anything to do with your profession. Therefore, this forces us to think that many complaints would not have been filed had there been some display of good manners from the doctor. Just like in the scenarios in chapter 1, it is important to remember that if you upset the wrong person in a hospital or office setting, that person may know that the hospital and your medical board have the ability to crush your career. If someone is upset with you for whatever reason, a complaint to the medical board is often the best weapon to use against you as a physician licensed by that medical board. The same thing goes for a hospital; your privileges to practice there could be revoked on the heels of a complaint and/or grievance from a hospital staff person who you rubbed the wrong way. There are some doctors who believe that they may have the behavior of what appears to be the perfect gentleman or lady to that hospital staffer—but that very fact combined with your success in that hospital may irk them, and jealousy may be enough to get them to formulate a plan to unleash the complaint from hell against you. This type of planning on the part of that individual can be a well-laid trap for an unsuspecting doctor. How can this happen, you ask? Sometimes the act of not noticing someone beside you is an unconscionable sin. Uplifting people who work with you and who enhance your ability to practice good medicine is a sign of great manners that could help avoid a potential complaint.

One way to help you think broadly about what it means to practice good manners as a physician or medical professional is to consider all the different people who could file a complaint against you. We mentioned briefly in the previous segment a few people who could file a complaint in addition to patients, such as hospital personnel. So, again, it is not just patients who file complaints. As I pointed out earlier, it could also be...

- family or friends of a patient
- office staff
- hospital staff
- a fellow physician
- a present or ex-employer
- a competitor
- a medical center, hospital administration, or peer group
- a payor/insurance organization
- a current or ex-spouse, girlfriend, or boyfriend

Suppose, for example, that you leave one hospital for another. Instead of giving your employer at the hospital ample notice of your departure and thanking him or her for the opportunities you had working there, you simply say, "I'm outta here." The people involved may be angered by that, believing they deserved more appreciation and respect from you. They might be upset about all the money they will lose when you go to another hospital. They might think that if you aren't going to make millions of dollars for them, then they don't want you to make it anywhere, certainly not for a competitor hospital across town.

What's more, former employers will often know how best to hurt you because they've worked with you for so long. During that time, they've seen that you weren't always perfect. They also have access to all your medical records, and they may be able to find something damaging in the medical records of your patients—if your poor manners motivate them to look for a problem there. So why give them the motivation? A situation like this could potentially be avoided if you take the time to gracefully make your exit, thanking your former employers for all they've done for your career, giving them credit for helping you get to where you are today, and maybe even offering to stay until they can find a replacement so that there isn't a loss of income. Thinking about how your actions are going to affect other people doesn't mean you have to give up a great opportunity. It just means that it's a good idea to be respectful and aware. Simply saying "sayonara" is probably not the best approach.

Dr. Cornered

Let me introduce you to another fictitious doctor, Dr. Cornered, who had a complaint filed against him by an ex-employee of his practice. The employee was a medical assistant who had been laid off and given severance. But what this employee really wanted was more money from the doctor, and he used a complaint as leverage.

When Dr. Cornered reached out to his attorney, he said, very nervously, "My former medical assistant demanded that I give him a boatload of money when he left, but I said no. He knows that I'm scared of having a complaint filed against me because I've talked about my fear of it so often at the office. So after I said no, he uttered the words 'complaint' and 'medical board.' Should I pay him off? What should I do?" He was advised that this situation could end right away with proper mediation and a strong stance to not be led by fear—or it could end in a complaint in which he would, hopefully, prevail.

This is an example of a situation where there was *not* any bad medicine. There was not even overtly bad behavior on the part of the doctor. Sometimes you can have the best bedside manner in the world but be up against plain . . .

evil. But even in such instances, a doctor's good behavior is still very relevant in the resolution of the complaint. It's times like that when I tell the doctor, "Remember who you are. Remember that you're a good doctor. No matter what the employee does, you've done nothing wrong, and your past record will show that. At the end of the day, you'll be exonerated." Because Dr. Cornered was both a good doctor and a good person, he had lots of people willing to speak for him. He had a record to show the medical board that he was proud of. And at the end of the day, he was indeed exonerated.

Even in this case, where Dr. Cornered clearly should not have received a complaint, and where he was clearly a good person and good doctor, he was counseled to examine his own behavior and consider whether there was something about his manner that he might adjust in the future to help avoid another complaint. He could have acted more professionally by not disclosing to his office staff that he had this unwarranted, persistent fear of the medical board. Maybe if he had kept a more professional demeanor and had not let his staff see his vulnerabilities, then this ex-employee wouldn't have thought to file the complaint. This is the kind of nuance with regard to good manners that is important to think about.

Unprofessional Conduct

Doctors should think broadly not just about who might file a complaint against them but also about what the nature of the complaint could be. The range of things that can cause a physician to be disciplined are pretty broad for most state medical boards, so I use the term "manners" to encompass a lot of things. For example, there is the "unprofessional-conduct rule." I always call that rule the "kitchen-sink rule" because it's thrown out there in so many cases.

When doctors are accused of unprofessional conduct, the first thing they usually say is, "How dare they say I was unprofessional? I'm always a professional." They're more offended by the word "unprofessional" than they are about practically anything else. But the term actually doesn't mean what they think it means. Generally, it means that they've violated rules and regulations in some way. That, in and of itself, it could be viewed as unprofessional because this conduct allegedly took place while they were practicing in their profession. That is my take on how "unprofessional" is defined, practically, in my clients' cases.

Doctors might be accused of being unprofessional because they failed to respond in a timely way to communications from a patient. Or because they kept poor records. Or because the doctor has terrible handwriting when writing prescriptions or notes in the record. Or because something they said in a personal conversation with a friend was overheard by a staff member who took offense to it.

So it's not necessarily unprofessional in the sense of a doctor's bad behavior—although it could mean that as well. This ambiguity is something that should be of concern to doctors because if the complaint does enter the public record and that language of "unprofessional behavior" is in it, laypeople looking at it will tend to imagine something much worse than just poor bookkeeping or handwriting.

For me, such minor lapses still fall under the heading of good manners because these are those little things that can still make a big difference to someone. An unintentional comment can hurt someone's feelings. Poorly written instructions or prescriptions can negatively impact communication. And poor records certainly have the potential of affecting patient care.

Falsification Rule: Dr. Loose Lips

A lot of doctors, when they attempt get their medical license, may fail to mention something in their application because, hey, it's been ten years or more since their residency, and they simply forgot about it. Or maybe they don't mention it because they didn't think it was a big deal in the first place. Of course, the board then collects all of that doctor's records, all the way back to medical school and continuing up to the present time. They're going to be examined to see if the doctor violated any board regulations or was disciplined by other states they were licensed in.

If you've been out of medical school and residency for ten years, you may not remember that you were late showing up one day when you were on call, and that you stubbed your toe while rushing in the door, and that in doing so you uttered some expletive that a nurse was offended by. That nurse may have then said to your supervisor, "Dr. Loose Lips is using profanity in the hallway." You might have responded by saying, "I'm sorry, you're right. I stubbed my toe and I was running late, but I shouldn't have said it. It won't happen again." And that was that—or so you thought—so you forgot about it. But maybe your supervisor went into your record and wrote, "Dr.

Loose Lips had a complaint filed by a nurse, who said he uses profanity in the workplace."

You may not even have known that your supervisor recorded the incident, but when you file an application for licensure in a new state and they pull all of your records, guess what they find? On the form you had to fill out, it asked "Have you ever been disciplined and/or warned in your residency and/or medical school?" You said no, but when the medical board sees this excerpt of a warning in your record, they send you an email saying, "You failed to mention that you were warned or reprimanded for using profanity." They call that falsification.

That kind of charge can come as a complete surprise to a doctor seeking licensure. Being false or deceptive was never their intention. We address this issue in other parts of the book, but it is important to know how these circumstances can arise. Who would have thought that something that started with stubbing one's toe years ago could amount to a complaint that a doctor would have to answer for years later? This is a fictitious scenario that shows the importance of doing your very best to be conscious of your actions and their consequences. Certainly, once something like this is revealed to have been the simple root of an issue, it is easily explained and understood and the doctor will fare well. And now, for these reasons, there is yet another layer of issues for you to deal with because now the board has technically caught you in a lie or false report. You might be this wide-eyed, bushy-tailed doctor, so excited to start an amazing job at a big hospital, and then all of a sudden you get accused of falsifying your record.

Honesty and integrity are obviously essential to having good manners, but for physicians the bar is set quite high. Of course, the board is not going to automatically disqualify you for state licensure because you made a mistake on your application, but they will expect you to own up to that mistake and take what happened seriously. And I believe it's fair for them to have such high standards for practicing physicians. I don't know of a single patient out there who would want it any other way.

Setting Boundaries: Dr. Friendly

I beg your pardon for the following words, but if you are a jerk with a horrible bedside manner, someone who's cruel or unfeeling toward people, that is really a recipe for disaster, not only in your medical career but in life, period. You are practically asking to see your career destroyed. But there's also the other side of the coin, where a physician can be *too nice*. Maybe you think, *I'm the nicest guy in the world. I'm the kindest, most compassionate physician for my patients. No one would ever complain about me.* If so, then maybe you are simply too nice, which just invites people to take advantage of you.

This might be a problem, for example, for a physician who treats chronic pain and regularly prescribes pain medication. Many of the pain doctors I've known are the nicest doctors in the world because they tend to have to high levels of compassion toward suffering people. But they must not be so kind that they end up writing prescriptions for patients who just shouldn't have them because that can get them into trouble.

To give another example, I would not want a doctor who is too "compassionate and kind" to want to cause me the discomfort of slicing into me to take out the tumor that's going to kill me. Do not be so careful and sweet that you are timid. Admittedly, that example may be pretty out-there, and you, I hope, would not run into it in the real world. But personally, faced with the prospect of being operated on by a surgeon with a timid, unsure nature, I'd say, "Get me a cocky, sure-handed doctor who will slice and dice on a dime while playing rock music in the operating room." I look for compassion, surely, but also experience and talent—and even some ego from knowing they are great at what they do. Kindness is important, but it needs to be balanced against other important qualities.

Dr. Friendly is everyone's favorite, every kid's godfather, and has delivered every baby in the county. That can easily happen in a very rural area. He forgets that his staff are professionals working in a healthcare facility and that his patients are his *patients*—not just his friends in a clinical setting. Thus he sets himself up for a potentially dangerous situation—because it is possible to be nice and kind to the point where it becomes unprofessional. Keeping the lines clear between the professional and the personal in an office setting and keeping feelings in check also count as good manners, but they tend to be the kinds of things that many people forget to consider. There has to be a patient-physician boundary that is strong enough not to be pierced. And there has to be a professional-personal boundary in any office or hospital setting.

Boundaries can mean anything from staying away from personal relationships with patients to not bartering for services. Now, there are still small towns in the United States with sweet country doctors who make house calls and walk out with a chicken in a bag instead of money for their services. There are towns where you can't throw a stone without hitting somebody who is your patient, so inevitably, you will go out to dinner with those same people or have them over to your house. But, generally, these are things that are frowned upon and should be avoided if possible. Another boundary that should go without saying, but is crossed so often that I feel I should say it, is that you shouldn't have sex with your patients. Period. Exclamation point!

At the end of the day, the good doctor who sets proper boundaries will survive a complaint a whole lot better than the one who doesn't.

Timeliness

As a physician or healthcare provider, you are in service to others. You should always be respectful to the people you're caring for and the people you're working with every day. When it comes to being respectful, one consideration that is too often overlooked in the medical profession is being *timely*. That means responding quickly to calls from patients or colleagues, particularly when you are on call. That means being on time for appointments as often as you possibly can. Of course, sometimes doctors can't do this because emergencies arise. A gynecologist, for example, might be anywhere from a few minutes to hours late if they're delivering a baby, so patients will have to sit in the waiting room or be rescheduled. But you can be respectful even in such cases. You can be apologetic and explain the situation so that patients understand that there's a good reason why they've been kept waiting. You can also give them an option to reschedule if the wait will be too long. Most of the time, that consideration and respect is all a patient needs to avoid frustration and a potential complaint.

You also need to train your staff to be an extension of yourself and to be just as kind and respectful as you are, especially in your absence. If you're dealing with an emergency, you may not be able explain the situation yourself to the patients you've kept waiting. In such instances, your staff needs to know how to apologize to the patients and explain what's happening so that the patients won't feel like they've been forgotten.

Being prompt, timely, and respectful fosters good patient care and good patient relationships. It also enhances your reputation with fellow healthcare providers, who will come to think of you as a reliable person. Timeliness is difficult for a lot of doctors today, given the pressures of their jobs, but it is still something they should strive for every day.

Checking Your Ego

Arrogance can come from great success. Doctors who are truly gifted may have reason to be arrogant because they've always stood out and have never made a mistake. It's not until they get knocked off that pedestal, sometimes with just a minor complaint, that they understand the importance of checking their ego.

Another aspect of manners that's important to think about is the fact that everyone is fallible. That includes even the most talented and successful doctors in the world, even the doctors who invented lifesaving procedures or found the cure for the worst disease of the century, and yes, even you, whoever you are.

Ego can get in the way of a lot of things that are essential to being the best doctor you can be. It can stop you from fully listening to a patient because you think you already know what's wrong. It can keep you from fully explaining instructions to a recovering patient or a nurse because you believe they should already know what you're talking about. Ego can also stop you from seeing or admitting to your mistakes when they happen, and that's a perfect recipe for ensuring that they will happen again. It also makes it hard for people to trust you, be it the patient who is putting his or her life in your hands, fellow physicians and health-care providers you work with, or boards and agencies that govern your practice or certifications. These people can decide and seal your fate.

CHAPTER 3:

The Negative Impact of Bad Manners

I've already talked about how the best way to handle a complaint is to avoid having one filed against you in the first place. Having good manners goes a long way toward doing that. But just avoiding complaints isn't the only reason to have good manners. It's not even the best reason. In this chapter, I will describe the wide range of negative impacts that bad manners can have on you and those around you. Bad manners will not just adversely affect you and your career as a physician; they can also have a negative impact on your patients, your patients' families, the people you work with, and even the people close to you in your own family. The risk of a complaint is just one part of what's at stake here.

Patient Health: Dr. Wounded

Things that we consider bad manners, like not taking the time to really listen to and observe a patient, can do more than just make that person feel hurt and disrespected. It can actually lead to poor patient outcomes that have a real negative impact on the lives of your patients.

For example, if a doctor doesn't care enough or is too rushed to give proper instructions to a patient upon discharge, that can be a big problem if, say, the patient needs to observe a wound and look for signs of infection. Or maybe the doctor does give instructions that the patient doesn't fully understand—but the doctor doesn't notice or doesn't care. Or the doctor doesn't fully listen to a patient who's describing his or her symptoms, which can lead to a misdiagnosis. Many of these problems can be lessened or avoided if a doctor simply practices good manners when it comes to communication.

When a doctor communicates with a patient, he or she should try to ensure that the patient feels comfortable enough to be forthcoming and to ask questions when necessary. That takes some time and effort. It means the doctor can't rush through an exam. It means the doctor has to be a good listener. It means the doctor with an arrogant attitude needs to check himself so that he doesn't make the patient feel uncomfortable about asking what might be perceived by the patient as a dumb question. It means having the kind of friendly and caring demeanor that invites rather than shuts down open and honest communication.

The thing to remember is that it's not a level playing field. You've probably heard the expression "God complex." That's often how a patient perceives his or her doctor. Most people have a great amount of respect for their physicians, and some may even view them in such a deferential way that they are afraid to speak up or ask questions. They're given directions, and they want to say "Yes, sir"—even if they don't fully understand what's been said. They might be afraid to come across as disrespectful to the doctor, so they just nod their head and walk out. As a physician, it's important to take personal responsibility for the quality of communication between you and your patients in order to ensure the best possible outcome for the patients' health.

Let's look at Dr. Wounded for an example of someone who was emotionally scarred by a tragedy in his personal life, was having a hard time sleeping, and was more distracted than usual. Naturally, that affected his professional life as well.

One day during this period, a patient was left to linger in the ER when what he really needed was to be transferred to a nearby hospital where he could receive a higher level of care. The hospital he was in just wasn't equipped to handle his condition, but that determination wasn't made in a timely manner, and the transfer didn't happen as quickly as it could have. As a result, the patient died. Dr. Wounded happened to be the physician who was called in because the physician who was actually on call could not be reached. Because he was the only doctor there, Dr. Wounded was blamed for this tragic outcome.

This is an especially tragic example of poor communication because once Dr. Wounded was made aware of the situation with this patient, he had quickly communicated the need for the transfer! He was the only physician in the ER that day, and it was packed with patients. The overwhelmed staff received the directive from Dr. Wounded to have the patient transferred but failed to do so, probably because of distraction from the patient load that evening. Plus, unfortunately, Dr. Wounded failed to document his directive to the nurse in the patient record because he was tired and stressed. He also harbored resentment for the missing on-call doctor and secretly felt that the blame should fall to that doctor. He was merely the treating physician called in because of the emergency situation.

To make matters worse, he had lately been mishandling the personal pain in his life by lashing out at others. He was known to be rude to the nurses, who regularly felt disrespected by him. Probably because of that, the directive he gave to the nurse to transfer the patient to another hospital was not jotted down in the nurse's notes, either. Or perhaps the nurse was so anxious to get away from Dr. Wounded before he could say something rude to her, that she didn't take the time to make thorough notes.

Dr. Wounded was then accused of misdiagnosing the severity of the patient's injuries. Only through a close examination of the records was it determined that he had, indeed, given the directive to transfer the patient. After much effort, his legal team discovered another doctor's notes and learned of phone calls made by Dr. Wounded to the higher-level hospital inquiring whether they had the appropriate facilities and available space and confirmed that they would accept the patient and prepare for the transfer and necessary treatment.

Still, Dr. Wounded never followed through to make sure the directive happened, nor did he nor the nurse keep a record of it. The nurse also wasn't willing to stick her neck out for Dr. Wounded and give evidence on his behalf, most likely due to the way he had treated her in the past. Dr. Wounded was exonerated at the end of the day regarding his treatment of the patient and taking the proper measures to transfer, but a patient still lost his life. And that happened in part because of the bad feelings and poor communication that occurred between him and hospital staff. There was no black mark left on his professional record, but one still has to wonder if—had he displayed a better attitude toward his coworkers and paid closer attention to them and their actions—the tragedy could have been avoided entirely.

This is a dramatic example, of course, but poor communication can absolutely have a negative effect on a patient's health. And sometimes it's an effect that you won't get the chance to correct, like injury or death.

Patient Well-Being: Dr. Bad News

That "God complex" I referred to earlier is the reason we have rules that govern doctor-patient boundaries and relationships. It's an uneven playing field, which is why it's inappropriate to ask to have sex with a patient or even ask one out on a date. I hope that many of you having just read this are saying, "Everyone knows that." You would be surprised to find out that, no, not everyone does.

You have power over your patients, much like a boss has over his or her employees, so it is not fair to say, "Will you go out with me?" and expect that the patient will feel comfortable turning you down, if that is what they really want to do.

I sometimes hear doctors say that this ban is extreme, that people can find love even in the examining room—but suppose you are the only physician who has ever truly treated the patient's ailment. For the first time, that patient can walk without pain. Then you ask the patient out. The individual might worry that you would stop treating them if he or she said no, thus subjecting him or her to chronic pain again. That is just one reason why it's so inappropriate. How could you ever know that the relationship is just about love or attraction when the patient says yes to you?

The same consideration for a person's well-being needs to happen when communicating bad news to someone, whether to patients themselves or to a member of a patient's family. You can cause or magnify someone's mental anguish when you deliver bad news in a cold, unfeeling way. Everyone dreads the tests we have to take as we get older in life. Many people are scared to death to hear a doctor's diagnosis. Doctors know this, or they should know it, and they should put themselves in the patient's shoes when delivering difficult news.

Over the course of my career, I have represented numerous doctors who, unfortunately, delivered news in a bad way. I've known doctors to say things like, "You have cancer and only six weeks to live. I'll leave you now so that you can share this with your family and start getting your affairs in order."

Now, you might say, "Well, that was the truth," but it's all in how the truth was delivered. The patient's complaint in this instance was that the doctor delivered the news in the presence of everyone in the hospital room, instead of in private, which could be a violation of the federal Health Insurance Portability and Accountability Act (HIPAA)[4]. It turned out that the people in her room were the doctor, the nurse, and her husband, so there was no actual violation— but the doctor was so callous in his delivery that the patient

4   You can find more information on HIPAA at www.hhs.gov/hipaa/. You can find more information on the Affordable Care Act at www.healthcare.gov.

was looking for a reason to complain. He spent less than two minutes to tell her she was dying. Given that, it's not surprising that he ended up on the receiving end of the complaint. Chances are that he could have avoided the complaint if he had just spent a couple more minutes holding the patient's hand and telling her how sorry he was.

To give another example, Dr. Bad News walked in to see a patient and, in a nonchalant way, said, "Well, I've got good news and I've got bad news. The bad news is you need surgery. The good news is I'm a great surgeon. Because I hear you're a woman of faith, the worst thing that can happen is that you die and then spend the rest of eternity in heaven with Jesus." You can just imagine how the patient felt about that doctor's attitude. In cases similar to this particular scenario, the patients didn't file complaints, but certainly could have. And all because of a bad joke made at a bad time.

As a doctor, you sometimes have to deliver bad news. That's simply part of the job. But you can always choose to do it with compassion and kindness. You can choose to spend a few extra minutes with the patient instead of giving the news and then running from the room. You may be uncomfortable about what you have to tell someone, but always remember that it's worse for them to hear it. And never deliver a bad joke just to mask your discomfort.

Workplace Relationships

I talked earlier about how a physician's rude and belligerent behavior toward hospital staff could have contributed to the death of a patient. That's an extreme example, but one that nonetheless could happen to any physician whose attitude makes people want to avoid him. That's a dangerous situation for the patient as well as the doctor. If people are trying to avoid you, you may not get all the information you need. You may not be called quickly enough when there's an emergency. And when a complaint is filed, even if it isn't your fault, you may have no one willing to stand up for you.

I've seen situations where a nurse who needs to consult a doctor about her patient calls the charge nurse instead because she's afraid to talk to that doctor. If it's an emergency situation, that wastes valuable time, which may harm the patient. Even if the patient isn't in danger, that's the kind of reputation that any doctor should be trying to avoid. Such things can end up in your record and lead to losing privileges at that hospital. It can make it harder for you to get a job in the future. It can make it harder to get licensed in another state. It can leave you open to complaints if something goes wrong. And it can just make your workday less efficient and less pleasant all around.

Keeping a collegial relationship with the people you work with is important, but I think it's especially important with nurses. The last person you should hurt in a hospital setting is the nurse because that's the person who should have your back, and that's the person who generally has the most contact with your patients. Doctors who are disrespectful to nurses, who see nurses as subordinates to be ordered around or as interchangeable tools instead of as individuals, those are the doctors who are going to find themselves on a spit turning over a hot fire. I was once told that if anyone knows how to hurt a physician, it's a nurse. Therefore, be kind and professional to your medical colleague.

Your Professional Reputation: Dr. Untouchable

At the end of the day, these kinds of situations can do serious damage to a doctor's reputation, even if they don't end up in a complaint. I've worked with doctors who have been truly blessed with extraordinary talent, leading to very successful careers. Some would say they were blessed with good luck in every aspect of their lives. They've been lucky all their lives, and no one has ever questioned them or criticized them. They are truly excellent physicians who are so good at what they do that the administration of their hospital is only too happy to look the other way when complaints arise. After all, these doctors are making millions of dollars for them and bringing great attention to the hospital. These are the kinds of doctors who often think they're untouchable and who are the most thrown when a complaint finally comes back to haunt them.

Doctors who have godlike personalities like Dr. Untouchable anger patients who just don't care how great they are. In this scenario, a patient doesn't realize that Dr. Untouchable is the doctor who invented something extraordinary in the medical community and is not afraid to say, "This guy was so rude to me. He came into my room and barely spoke to me. And when he did, he was cold and dismissive."

A doctor may be able to get away with being aloof and arrogant for a time because of his reputation, but even the best doctors are putting themselves in danger by acting this way. It can take only one complaint for the walls to come crashing down. After that one patient who doesn't care about Dr. Untouchable's greatness complains about him, then other healthcare providers who have worked with him throughout the years might start coming out of the woodwork. They held their tongues before because the hospital prized this doctor so much, but now they get a chance to say what they've always wanted to say, which is that he's rude and arrogant and treats them terribly.

Complaints have a way of growing legs and gaining momentum. If a complaint starts to snowball, especially if it's against a high-profile doctor, then local news reporters might be called. They might see a great story about Dr. Untouchable falling from his pedestal.

Then guess what happens? This doctor, who's been so arrogant, who got away with such nasty behavior for so long, has become too high-profile for the hospital to stand behind him any longer. Before, the administration protected him, but now they are saying, "Whoops, you're bad news."

In addition, as I mentioned before, it's the age of the Internet. Any bad report about a doctor can be recorded for all time for anyone to find with a simple web search. Even if the case doesn't make the news, there are all sorts of outlets where a person can voice a complaint. And that's the case even if the bad news isn't true or isn't the whole story. These things can stick to you. In this day and age, no one is truly untouchable.

So often the negative consequences that I've talked about in this chapter can be avoided with simple good manners. What's worse, in my view, is that bad manners may cause you to miss out on all the good things that good manners can bring. That's what I will discuss in the next chapter.

CHAPTER 4:

The Positive Impact of Good Manners

Avoiding complaints and other negative consequences is a big reason to cultivate good manners, but it's far from the only, or even the best, reason. This chapter will describe some of the positive impacts that good manners can have on various aspects of your professional and your personal life.

Patient Health and Welfare

I have often heard from patients that the fact that their physician had a caring disposition and genuinely wanted them to get better made a big difference to them in their recovery and healing. I talked in the last chapter about the power difference between a doctor and a patient. When someone looks up to an individual and holds him or her in high esteem, it is only natural that he or she wants to please that person. So if patients know that their health and healing is important to their physician, they often aspire to meet the physician's goals. The power of mind over matter is something that there has been ample research on.

I have had physicians tell me they will pray with their patients, or they will let their patients know they are praying for them. That can be very important to patients of faith, making them feel like the physician respects their faith and that he or she cares enough to keep them in prayer. The power of prayer itself has been well documented as a source of healing. Of course, physicians can't make miracles, and patients shouldn't expect them to, but doctors still have a profound ability to give a person hope. And there's a great power in hope, whether or not the physician is a person of faith. You can bring hope to a patient through prayer or simply with words, by telling the patient you believe he or she can recover (if it is still within the realm of possibility) and that you will do everything you can to make it happen. Your confidence and kindness can impart a real sense of peace in a patient who is facing something frightening. It is important to note at this point that this does not excuse the responsibility that this physician would have in fully informing the patient of what the prognosis is. But deciding to believe and sharing your belief and hope with the patient that it is possible to defy the odds is so encouraging and meaningful for your patient, who has expressed their belief in the fight.

Improved Communication with Patients: Dr. Sandman

The thing that should be in the forefront of any physician's mind is the welfare of the patient. When patients allow you to treat them, they're putting their life in your hands. When that happens, they're in a vulnerable position, so the first thing they want is to feel safe. To help them feel that way, the first words coming out of your mouth should have a note of kindness as well as certainty. Being kind helps patients feel at ease, and being certain and confident gives them a sense of security and trust. This will put them in the right mindset and help them feel comfortable communicating openly with you and giving you a full picture of what's happening with their health.

Of course, good communication isn't just about how you talk to your patient; it's also about how you listen to him or her. As the patient is relaying critical information, you should show that you're truly observing and listening without distraction. You can convey that by making eye contact, offering nods of assurance, asking questions about what's been said, and indicating that you understand his or her concerns.

Let me introduce you to my next character, Dr. Sandman, who found himself in a lot of trouble because he had a habit of closing his eyes while listening to patients. Patients found that very off-putting, and when a patient finally filed a complaint, the first charge was that Dr. Sandman had fallen asleep during their consultation. The physician had not fallen asleep, but his habit of closing his eyes gave that impression. In order to exonerate this physician, his legal team had to come up with affida-vits stating that this was how he normally behaved, that he regularly closed his eyes so that he could be an intent listener.

I don't tell this story to suggest that everyone should interact in the exact same way with patients. Doctors are individuals, after all, with different backgrounds, experi-ences, and habits, and that's the way it should be. What I *am* suggesting is that you consider how your particular quirks might affect communication with your patients. Dr. Sandman could have saved himself a lot of trouble if he had just taken the time to explain himself to his patients. He could have said, "I really want to listen to what you have to say without missing a thing, so I'm going to close my eyes so I don't have any distractions." The same could be said of doctors who like to take copious notes and therefore rarely look up from their charts. The lack of eye contact could be perceived by a patient as being impersonal or inattentive, but any such misunderstanding can be cleared up with a simple explanation.

What this boils down to is having self-awareness of your communication style so that you can mitigate any aspects that might turn off or offend your patients. Put yourself in the shoes of the other person, and try to be aware of how you're affecting him or her. In order to do this, you have to observe the person you're speaking with. We are living in an age when everybody is connected to phones or other devices, but when it comes to communicating effectively with another human being, there's nothing more effective than being in the moment so that you can really pay attention to what's happening.

Improved Communication with Family Members and Friends

Good communication is essential when dealing with patients *and* with the people who accompany those patients to the office or hospital—usually their family members or friends. Some physicians feel that if there's another party in the room, they don't have to work as hard to communicate with their patients, because that second party can help translate what they're trying to get across. But I don't believe that's correct. When you're dealing with more than one person in the room, you need to try even harder.

If a patient brings someone else to his or her appointment, you should always acknowledge the presence of that person and do so in a friendly and respectful way. Introduce yourself and show gratitude that they took the time to escort your patient to your office. As you continue to talk, you should keep in mind that you're dealing with two different personalities, each receiving the information that you're relaying in different ways.

From a legal perspective, this is where taking accurate notes and having a proper medical record becomes especially valuable, because you've now got a "witness" in the room who can back up any claims made by the patient. You may even want to have a medical assistant or nurse as your wing person in the room so that you have your own witness if a complaint is filed. Of course, as I've said before, the best defense against a complaint is to not get one in the first place, which is why it's particularly important to display good manners toward everyone in the room, including the patient's friends and family.

Another reason to pay particular attention to the people accompanying your patient is that they are the ones likely to assist in the care of that patient if anything critical happens. Many times it's the caregiver who will be caring for a wound after surgery or administering medications. That means that friends or family members need to be put in a comfortable, receptive mode in order to properly hear and understand your instructions. They need to feel comfortable enough to ask questions. If you are being rude, if you ignore them, or if you rush through the delivery of important information, it can make the patient's advocate feel like he or she cannot talk to you. That can lead not only to ill feelings toward you but also to mistakes in the care of your patient once the patient leaves the hospital or examining room.

Getting Back What You Give: Dr. Manners and Dr. Coldheart

Practicing good manners makes it more likely that people will treat you with good manners in return. It can also make it less likely that someone will file a complaint against you, even if you *have* made a mistake. We all make mistakes at some point—after all, we are all human. But whether or not you will be forgiven for your mistake has to do in large part with how the person doing the forgiving feels about you.

I told a story earlier in this book about a doctor who was blamed in a patient's serious outcome. In this similar scenario, there were multiple physicians responsible for the unfortunate patient's care, and this particular physician, who we will call Dr. Coldheart, wasn't even the primary one. So why would he get the blame when others may not? In a situation like this one, some families may not blame Dr. Manners, who could be the one most likely to be at fault, because they really *liked* Dr. Manners. He had been really kind to them, had talked with them often, and had told them how sorry he was when the patient passed away. Dr. Coldheart, in contrast, could have had a more businesslike, no-nonsense personality. He spent very little time talking to the patient's family and hadn't bothered to offer his condolences to them after they had lost their loved one. So guess who the family blamed at the end of the day? Dr. Coldheart, of course.

To make Dr. Coldheart's situation worse, when the complaint was filed, can you guess whether or not he had the support that Dr. Good Manners would have had if he had received a complaint? Considering his "cold personality", Dr. Coldheart had fewer friends, and even a few enemies, because of the way he treated people. That put him in a bad position. Dr. Manners, on the other hand, has always been well liked and could have easily found nurses or fellow doctors who would testify positively about him, were he to be named in such a complaint. This positive feedback would come because, not only was he a very good doctor, but he had always treated them with respect and kindness.

Better Work Environment

Good manners help create a more positive work environment for you and for the people around you. If you say "good morning" to the people around you when you arrive each day, if you make a point of saying "thank you" to those who help you out, if you adopt good habits like the ones I've been talking about, then you can help to create a much more pleasant place to go to work every day. Simple acts of kindness and basic good manners can really have an impact. If you think about how many hours most physicians work, being in a happier, more positive environment could have a real impact on their lives.

Think about how nice it feels when a patient sits up in bed when you walk in the room, smiling at you and thanking you for making them better. The feeling of doing good for others makes you a happier, healthier person. The people around you want to feel good, too, and you can help with that by being appreciative and thankful of their contributions. When everyone feels good about what they're doing and the people they work with, it can decrease the stress level all around. That can only help you enjoy your job more.

Some people define a hospital as a "house of death," but it doesn't have to be seen that way. Every person in that hospital has the power to breathe life into the place with his or her positive outlook and attitude so that people don't feel like they're going to a place to die. Instead, they're going to a place to get better, to heal, to recuperate, to walk out feeling more alive. You can breathe life into your patients, your patients' families and friends, and your fellow hospital staff if you choose to make how you treat them a priority in your daily life.

Better Career Options

All that good energy you put out into the world will come back to you. Not only will it lead to better patient outcomes and better relationships, it will lead to things like good ratings and reviews, more repeat business, and more referrals. Other doctors will entrust patients to you because of the good things they've heard about you. All in all, your reputation will precede you.

There's not one doctor out there who is perfect. Every doctor will have a bad outcome at some point, but not every bad outcome denotes bad medicine. Sometimes there are risk factors that the doctor cannot avoid. But if you find yourself in that position, people are much more likely to continue their treatment with you, regardless of the occasional bad outcome, because of the good reputation you've established and the good relationships you've developed.

Many times, the reason someone recommends you is not because you're absolutely brilliant but because of how you come across in the care you're giving. You may not have graduated from the best medical school, and some may even say that you are not the most talented, but if your personality conveys that good care is important to you and that you truly care about your patients, then you can still have a thriving practice.

We're living in a time where the impact you make on people is more and more important. People can register their thoughts or complaints either formally or on online review sites that all the world has access to. The other day I went to my primary-care physician, and afterward I was given a questionnaire (patient survey) that said, "Thank you for coming to our clinic today. Please take the next five minutes to rate your healthcare provider." That information may not be public, but I'm sure the clinic's administration takes note of it. Insurance companies that back physicians are also taking a greater interest in this kind of information because it gives them insight into who might be at greatest risk for a complaint. There can be great incentives that come along with these surveys.

This is really where good manners come full circle. Being good and kind and honest with people is not only good for them and good for the people around them, but it's also good for you. It will come back to you in a positive way. It improves your outcomes, it improves your working environment, *and* it improves your business—because people want to come to you or refer you or work with you. Patients have a lot of choice these days over where and from whom they receive care. Think about why a patient would choose you above all the other options out there.

CHAPTER 5:

When to Start Practicing Good Manners

My short answer to the question of when to start practicing good manners is quite simple: "Right away."

It's an unfortunate thing that good manners are not traditionally taught in medical school because that's when the practice and development of good manners should start—at least in a professional sense. Really, the development of good manners should start in childhood, but none of us can control who our parents were and whether such things were taught to us or not. If they weren't taught at home or addressed in a person's schooling, that person can actually get quite far in his or her career without thinking about manners. It is people like that who, all too often, only get their wake-up call when someone ultimately files a complaint against them. That's why it's so important for everyone to take the time to ask themselves what kind of people they are when they practice their craft and how they are affecting those around them.

With this in mind, the answer to when to start practicing good manners is "right now," in whatever moment you find yourself in. If you are new to the medical profession, this is the perfect time to establish good habits. If you've practiced for thirty years and you've never had good manners but have always been brilliant and respected, then you should know that you can only become better at what you do—and better shield yourself from risk—if you cultivate good manners now. Even if you have had a complaint filed against you, which is perhaps what opened your eyes to the need to do some things differently, you can still change bad habits. It's never too late to learn, and right now is always a good time to start.

Students and New Physicians: Dr. New-Body

Many students and young doctors don't realize that their behavior today can have a negative impact that will stick to them for many years to come. Dr. New-Body, for example, was a young doctor applying for a medical license. When such an application is filed, the medical board for the state reviews it, and if there are any red flags, they will investigate them. In this case, the medical board contacted the medical school that Dr. New-Body attended, and in her school record they discovered a notation about a disciplinary action that had taken place. It came as an absolute shock to this young physician that an incident of bad personal behavior while she was still in medical school had any relevance to the licensing medical board she applied to. But it did.

Your manners and how you carry yourself in medical school, as well as the impressions you make on your instructors, are very important—not just at the time, but potentially down the line when anyone has cause to review your professional record. For this particular young physician, the problem was simply a matter of her not showing up for classes. And, when there was an inquiry into her absences, she didn't respond, so she was put on academic probation. It wasn't because she wasn't smart but rather because she was overburdened. She had a schedule packed with classes as well as part-time employment to pay for them. But her behavior came across to her instructors as being disrespectful, and voila, she found herself on academic probation and had to repeat a semester. After that, she got her act together and graduated with honors. Later on, when she was getting ready to move to another state for a new job, her past came back to bite her. Again, we are using the story of a physician seeking a license who has to answer for their past/historical circumstances. I believe these scenarios are important for medical students to consider because it brings them to the moment of different scenarios that they may face early on and should consider the circumstances. She thought it was all behind her, but it wasn't. Dr. New-Body said to her attorney, "That happened six years ago. Can they really be making a big deal out of this?" The answer was yes, they can.

In this particular scenario, the doctor was able to explain to the board that this was *not* indicative of her usual behavior but rather something that happened during a difficult period in her life. Medical boards don't expect you to be faultless, but they will make you explain your faults and reassure them that you are, on the whole, worthy of the trust they put in you when they give you a license to practice. And they will pay particular attention to your behavior when you answer for those faults or red flags in your record. Are you arrogant and defensive, or do you take responsibility when you explain what happened? Do you come across as forthcoming and honest? Or are you trying to cover up or diminish what happened? Are you respectful of the board when you answer their questions? All these things matter.

If Dr. New-Body later applies for privileges at a new hospital or wants to join a new practice, those records from as far back as medical school could resurface. If a complaint is filed against her for showing up late to appointments or not responding quickly to emergency calls, they can show up again. The medical board might then look at the record and see a pattern of bad behavior, which began with that first silly incident back in medical school that she thought she'd put behind her.

I've had the good fortune of meeting some of the most brilliant medical and scientific minds out there, but upon my first meeting with many of them, I hear the same thing: "I can't believe anyone is making such a big deal out of this thing that happened. I'm a doctor, but this has nothing to do with medicine."

If we're honest with ourselves, we know that we're judged in this world on more than just the work we do. People are constantly judging the kind of people we are:

who we choose to associate with and under what circumstances, how we talk to people, whether we're honest and forthright, and whether we respect others and show up on time when possible. These are the kinds of things that people judge us on, and by people, I mean *all* people—our patients, our peers, our supervisors and administrators, and certainly the members of any medical board or jury. After all, if you were disrespectful to your teachers in medical school, why shouldn't we assume that you could be that way to your patients or colleagues later in life? If you cheated on a test back then, you might be the kind of person who would lie about whether you gave a patient accurate information. If you've been indiscreet about who you've had relationships with in your personal life, why wouldn't we think that you might be indiscreet about leaking patient information? It is your *behavior* that enables people to trust you, long before you have any chance to prove to them that you're a medical genius.

Educating Yourself on Proper Manners

Since this subject is generally not taught in all medical schools (though I think there's a strong argument to be made that it should be), it really is the responsibility of all professionals to educate themselves—and, in my view, to do so as early as possible because of all the reasons I've talked about so far.

If you're still in medical school, you can start by doing simple things: be respectful to your professors, show up to class on time, make an effort to listen carefully to people, and treat your fellow students with respect. You may be the best student in the class, but if you can't manage these rudimentary lessons that any grade schooler should be able to do, you could leave people wondering about you. If you're arrogant, disrespectful, and irresponsible, people will wonder whether those qualities might ultimately lead you to provide poor patient care. Because, if you're not a good listener, how are you going to diagnose patients on your own? If you're not respectful, how are you going to collaborate with other physicians who may have a different healthcare plan than you do?

If you need to brush up on your skills in the good manners department (and even if you don't), the following are some tips to get you started.

- Treat everyone with respect.
- Be a good listener.

- Show people that you've listened and that you care.
- Make an effort to be on time.
- Admit to your mistakes.
- Learn how to say "I'm sorry."
- Make a point of saying "thank you" often.
- Always aim to do the right thing.
- Keep your sex life and your professional life separate.
- Don't use profanity in the workplace.

Be Aware of Yourself and Your Environment: Dr. Delusional

Young doctors can practice the kind of observation skills that are critical to diagnosing patients by focusing those skills on themselves and their environment. Learning to really look at yourself and what's happening around you is a skill you will find useful for the rest of your life.

For example, sometimes when a doctor is accused of being rude or behaving badly, it simply comes down to cultural differences. I could take my southern belle self into the city of New York and have complete culture shock.

Or someone else might take a New York attitude into the countryside of Georgia and offend an entire town. That happens sometimes to doctors, especially young ones who find themselves in school or residency programs somewhere far from home. A doctor might be all about taking care of business while working in a culture where patients expect more small talk and common courtesy. That can translate into the doctor being unfeeling or even a jerk. It's understandable—but I would also say it's the responsibility of the doctors, with their keen observation skills, to pick up on cultural differences when they move to a new place and adjust their behavior accordingly.

What can be even more difficult for many doctors is for them to turn those powers of observation on themselves in a true and real way. Let's say Dr. Delusional felt the sole reason a complaint was filed against him was simply because the doctor behind the complaint was jealous of him. That does happen sometimes, so his attorney told Dr. Delusional that if that was truly the case, then at the end of the day he would be exonerated because of his good work and reputation.

Of course, you can probably guess that it wasn't someone else's jealousy that caused this complaint. It was the doctor's own poor behavior, which he was blind to. He was the kind of brilliant-but-arrogant doctor who just assumed everyone was jealous of his greatness because that's the way he saw himself. Often our true natures are revealed in difficult situations like the one this doctor was facing.

The question that all doctors—whether they are seasoned or just starting out—should be asking themselves is: Is this me? Is my arrogance getting in the way of me seeing reality? Am I blind to my faults? And how might that leave me vulnerable to complaints?

When I'm trying to assess the character of my clients, I often ask them questions like: Do you know the name of the lunch lady or janitor in your hospital, whom you walk by every day? Do you know whether or not the triage nurse is married and has children?

Some clients might say, "Why should I know such things? I'm trying to practice medicine here. I don't have time for things like that." Well, those people may very well have found the time to learn *your* name and also form an opinion about what you're like to work with. That nurse might think you're a jerk because you never respond to her pages, and that custodian might think you're rude. And one day they might have reason to file or contribute to a complaint because of what they think about you.

Because our own behavior can be difficult to assess fully and honestly at times, I'm going to talk more about this subject in chapter 7. There's even a quiz to help you diagnose whether or not you suffer from chronically bad behavior.

CHAPTER 6:

Correcting a Negative Event

Taking a proactive approach and adopting the kind of pleasant and professional manner that makes it less likely that someone would want to lodge a complaint against you is the best strategy for avoiding complaints. However, in my work, I have seen on too many occasions that it isn't always possible to avoid complaints, even with the best manners. So, if the worst *does* happen and someone files a complaint against you—warranted or not—this chapter will help you figure out what you can do about it.

Making a Mistake: Dr. Good Intentions

Every good doctor needs to be diligent and careful, but nonetheless, mistakes do happen. Even good doctors can make mistakes. Let's say Dr. Good Intentions, for example, performed a knee operation. The procedure went flaw-lessly, but when it was over, he became aware that he had operated on the wrong knee!

It happened, in part, because when Dr. Good Intentions visited the patient before the surgery to review what they were going to do, he asked the patient which knee they'd be operating on. The patient, either because of nerves or by simple mistake, pointed to his left knee when he should have indicated his right. The doctor then marked the left knee, and when he got into the operating room later that day, that was the knee he operated on.

Of course, Dr. Good Intentions *should* have consulted the patient's record, his X-rays and other scans, and the radiology report before performing surgery—so even though the patient indicated the wrong knee, the physician was still responsible. In this case, the patient had been a longtime athlete, so both his knees had some wear and tear (which is the reason Dr. Good Intentions didn't notice anything was amiss when he was performing the surgery). However, one knee was in worse shape than the other, and the patient had decided to have the worse knee operated on first so that he'd have the use of the better leg while he recovered. Of course, if you're going to be using only one knee for a time and putting extra strain on it, you'll want it to be the one that is in better shape.

Unfortunately, that wasn't how it worked for this patient. When he got out of surgery, he had to go through a painful recovery because of the added pressure being put on an already unhealthy joint. His other knee had practically disintegrated, so it made the recovery process that much more difficult for him. As a result, the patient filed a complaint.

As anyone in the medical profession knows, mistakes like this do happen. This mistake was an obvious one, but they aren't always this clear-cut. Sometimes the mistake can be something as simple as making a comment to a patient that was inappropriate or giving information to a patient's spouse when it was specified in the record not to do that (which could very well be considered a HIPAA violation). A doctor may argue that the first scenario is a much more serious mistake, and maybe it is, but for our purposes here, let's just call a mistake a mistake. Once you've made one, the real question is: What do you do about it?

Steps for Correcting a Mistake

Regardless of the nature of the mistake, if you are truly responsible, then steps must be taken to correct the mistake as much as possible and hopefully avoid further problems, like lawsuits or complaints. The basic steps are as follows:

Step 1: Admit the wrong. This means first admitting to yourself that it was your mistake, which is difficult for some doctors to do, and then admitting the mistake to the party that you've wronged.

Some people will read that and scream, "No, don't do that!"—because you're admitting to liability. But believe it or not, when a mistake is made, and it's obviously your fault, to hide from responsibility will often make matters worse, whereas if you apologize and own up to your mistake from the very beginning, it opens up the opportunity for forgiveness. The patient, or other party who has been harmed and feels hurt by the mistake, will only feel more injured and infuriated if he or she looks you in the eye and says, "Doctor, you did this to me," and you ignore it or skirt around the fact that you did indeed do it.

Over the course of my career, there have been many occasions where either a client or a physician I knew from the community says to me, "Victoria, I've made this mistake. What do I do?" It often shocks them when I respond by asking, "Well, what do you feel is the right thing to do, doctor? What does your heart tell you?"

Often they pause, and then say something like, "Oh gosh, I was afraid you would ask me that. To me, the right thing would be to admit what happened and apologize to the patient." That's when I typically say, "Well then, I would advise you to do what your gut is telling you. That is what will allow you to sleep at night."

Step 2: Apologize immediately. It's important not only to be clear about the mistake you've made and apologize for it, but to do so quickly, before matters get worse. This allows injured people to continue to trust you even though you've made a mistake. It allows them to feel like their judgment was not wrong in putting their faith in you, and they won't feel further violated or betrayed by a lie or cover-up.

When speaking to the patient, you have to be very fact based and informative, and avoid beating around the bush. Dr. Good Intentions, for example, would say something like: "Sir, the procedure itself went off flawlessly. However, a mistake was made in preparing for the surgery. When I asked you which knee we were operating on before surgery, you pointed to the left knee. However, the knee you intended for us to operate on was in fact your right. I take responsibility for this error, and I apologize for it. I should have consulted your records and made certain we had the correct knee before going into the operating room. I've already informed the hospital of my error, and we'll do what we can to make up for this mistake."

Often I will help doctors put just how they're going to apologize into the right words, because, believe it or not, some doctors just don't know how to apologize properly (more on that important subject later in this chapter).

Step 3: Take corrective action as best you can. When speaking to the patient, apologize first, and then tell him or her what you're going to do to correct or make up for your mistake. In the case of Dr. Good Intentions, he might go on to say, "I am not going to charge you for this procedure. I will pay out of pocket for the hospital services and fees as well, to make this up to you. And after you've healed from this surgery, I'll do your other knee free of charge if you'll let me. As I said, the surgery itself went off without a hitch, so I hope you'll trust me to do that so I can make this up to you. Again, I apologize profusely for what happened."

Conversations like this one are almost surely going to be difficult because these are not easy things for a patient to hear. People already feel vulnerable when they put their lives in a doctor's hands, and a mistake only magnifies that feeling. That's why it's important not only to admit clearly what you did and apologize for it but to offer compensation for your actions if possible. That could mean not charging for the procedure, paying for additional costs like hospital or recovery fees, or doing a corrective procedure.

Step 4: Understand why the mistake happened, and do what you can to ensure it won't happen again. You want to offer corrective actions if you can, but that's not always possible. In a scenario like the one I mentioned earlier, where you gave information to a patient's spouse that you shouldn't have, you can't take back those words. You can, however, apologize both to the patient and to the patient's spouse for putting them in a difficult position. You can also make sure you understand fully how the mistake happened. Then, as part of your apology, you can tell the injured party what steps you'll take to make sure this same mistake doesn't happen to them or anyone else in the future.

Consider a scenario where a patient feels that a member of the physician's staff had been very rude and abrasive to him while he was in the hospital. In that case, in addition to apologizing, the physician responsible for that patient's care assured him that not only would the staff member be disciplined, but that he would require the person to undergo behavior counseling to make sure this type of thing didn't happen to another patient.

Many times, mistakes are a result of some sort of systematic breakdown. There are supposed to be multiple checks to ensure a doctor is operating on the correct knee, for example. So why didn't those checks happen in this case? What additional checks should be put in place to make sure they don't happen again? Was there something about the doctor's communication with the patient that led to getting the wrong answer from him? These are the kinds of questions that responsible doctors with good manners need to ask themselves. What could I have done differently? What could those around me have done differently? How might the system function more effectively in the future?

The Power of Truth

As I mentioned earlier in this chapter, many people think that telling the truth is not the first thing a lawyer would suggest. People often think that admitting to any wrongdoing is the *last* thing they should do. However, there are real benefits to telling the truth.

First is the old adage that the truth will set you free. Once the truth is established, no one can ever catch you in a lie. And that's liberating because then all you have to deal with are the consequences of the truth, not on maintaining a lie or denial. I always tell people never to shackle themselves to a lie. It takes a lot of work to remember what you've said and keep your story consistent when it's not the truth. And that kind of stress is what keeps people up at night.

The second reason is to maintain your professional credibility. If, at the end of the day, you find yourself in front of the medical board defending yourself because of a mistake you made, you're only going to make matters worse for yourself if you also end up having to defend yourself for covering up or lying about the mistake. And I do believe that what happens in the dark generally comes to light. If someone owns up to a mistake right away, then the board can look at his or her behavior and past record and say, "Okay, this doctor took responsibility from the very beginning, and his track record outside of this incident is exemplary, so this is someone whom we can still trust." State medical boards and hospital review boards understand that doctors are human and that humans make mistakes, but if you lie about your mistake and they catch you, how can they have any confidence in you going forward? Doctors who lie are likely to lie in the future. And doctors who don't admit their mistakes are less likely to take the kinds of actions necessary to ensure they don't make a mistake again.

When I'm helping a client who has made a mistake prepare for a hearing, I always tell him or her, "Put the judges in your shoes at the time of the mistake. Even though you made this error, help them understand why it happened. Show them that you have done the work of understanding how it happened so that it doesn't happen again. I want them to see themselves in your shoes because, but for the grace of God, it could just as easily have been them making this type of mistake. You know you did something wrong, but you have the class, the forthrightness, and the professionalism to be honest about it and take it seriously."

Finally, telling the truth gives the person you've injured the opportunity to forgive you. The patient might be upset with you, but he can still respect you if you've been honest with him. But if he senses that you've lied or stretched the truth even a little, that patient will just get angrier and more upset because you have essentially wronged him a second time. He will feel further victimized, which is likely to make him want compensation all the more.

Doctors need to realize that when they make a mistake with a patient, that patient may not only get angry at them, but also at him or herself. Patients often become disappointed in themselves because they trusted you. They didn't see that you were a bad guy or a bad girl, and maybe they should have. But at the end of the day, if you make a mistake but act honorably in spite of it—by being truthful and remorseful—then that patient's faith, both in you and in his or her own instincts about you, can be restored.

The mistake you made may have been bad, but that doesn't mean you are a bad person. The defining moment comes in how you accept responsibility for your behavior, even if it means a negative outcome. After a mistake is made, we all have a choice of either lifting ourselves up or falling further down the hill. If we catch ourselves before we tumble all the way down, then we've avoided greater injury, haven't we?

How to Construct an Appropriate Apology

When it comes time for doctors to apologize for their actions, I've found far too often that they just don't know the right words. Maybe it's because they've been fortunate enough to have practiced for many years without making a mistake, or at least without a mistake that ended up on the record. Or maybe apologizing just isn't something they've ever learned to do. Whatever the case, when it comes to apologizing, it's important to do it right, or you can just make matters worse.

In order to construct an appropriate apology, you have to:

Say the words. Sometimes people have a tendency to beat around the bush, but if you want someone to understand that you're apologizing to them, you have to say the words. You can't just ramble on about the terrible thing that happened. You need to say "I'm sorry" or "I apologize."

Acknowledge what it is you're apologizing for. You can't *just* say, "I'm sorry." You need to say, "I'm sorry this mistake happened." You need to be specific about the mistake that was made and not hide behind generalities.

Make it clear that you're taking responsibility for what happened. The most common mistake that people make is to apologize by saying, "I'm sorry this happened to you." That's not the same as saying, "I'm sorry that *I played a part in causing this* to happen to you." The apology doesn't feel heartfelt or genuine if you don't make it clear that you understand and are acknowledging that you're at fault in some way.

Make sure you're apologizing to the right person. Believe it or not, I've had doctors say to me after making a grave error, "Well, I apologized to the hospital administrator for the mistake I made in the care of this patient." I then have to ask, "Did you ever actually apologize to the patient?" Far too often, the answer I get is "Well, no." Maybe it is appropriate to apologize to the hospital administrator as well— but you haven't fully done your job if you've overlooked the person who was injured the most by your actions.

Take a broad view of who has been affected by your actions. You also need to step back and consider everyone who has been affected by what you've done. If you operated on the wrong knee, which means the patient's wife has to spend more of her time and energy helping her husband recover, then you might owe her an apology as well. If you disclosed information to a patient's husband that you weren't supposed to, you certainly owe the patient an apology—but maybe you owe the husband an apology as well for putting him in a position where his wife got angry with him for knowing something she didn't want him to know. There may also be other physicians or staff members who got dragged into the mess, maybe even exposed to litigation, as a result of what happened. If that's the case, they're owed an apology as well.

After apologizing, make it clear what you're going to do to make up for your mistake and what you're going to do make sure the same mistake doesn't happen in the future. As I mentioned before, your responsibility doesn't end with "I'm sorry." You also have to try to make up for what you've done. And you have to learn from your mistake and allow it to help you become a better doctor in the future.

Instead of saying, "I apologize that your surgery went wrong," say, "I'm sorry I didn't follow through and look at the complete record before going ahead with the procedure. If I'd done that, this mistake wouldn't have happened, and I'm so very sorry for that."

Instead of: "It's unfortunate what happened with your husband," say, "I'm sorry that I spoke to your husband when I shouldn't have. You'd asked not to have any private information disclosed to him, and I should have looked more closely at the notes in the file before speaking to him."

A Written Apology

Sometimes physicians find themselves in a situation where they aren't able to apologize in person. In such cases, a written apology is something that should be strongly considered.

Suppose you're a physician who spoke unprofessionally in front of a patient, using what the patient considered to be vulgar language. You might barely remember the incident in question when a complaint is filed with the board later on. The board might say, "We understand how this mistake could have taken place. There really was no violation in the standard of care. However, you've acknowledged that you did speak these words and that you weren't careful about who might have been within earshot when you said them. Because someone was offended by what you said, we'll close this case under the condition that you write a letter of apology to the patient."

Even if the board isn't requiring one, a written apology can sometimes be the best thing you can do to smooth things over with a patient. For example, maybe you weren't made aware of a problem until the patient left your office, and now he or she isn't accepting your calls. If you don't have an opportunity to speak with somebody face-to-face, a written apology can be a good substitute. If you do it quickly and mean what you say, you may even stop someone from filing a complaint in the first place.

Often, when I first speak to a client about a complaint that has happened over some sort of personal issue (such as a poor choice of language or a patient feeling slighted because the doctor ignored him or her as he or she rushed out to an emergency), I'll ask, "Doctor, did you ever apologize to this patient?" "Well, no," is often the response, "but I wish I had. Because if I had, I probably wouldn't be sitting with you today." To which I'll say, "You're right. You probably wouldn't be."

Just because an injured or offended person doesn't make it easy for you to apologize doesn't mean you shouldn't follow through and make the effort all the same. Even if it doesn't make the person feel better and the matter does end up in a formal complaint, the board will appreciate that you attempted to resolve the situation responsibly rather than ignore it or sweep it under the rug.

More often than not, however, if you do reach out and apologize, people will be willing to forgive you. It can be awkward for patients to have to walk away from your office feeling offended or wronged in some way. They don't want to feel that way, but it's not always obvious how to resolve things productively. When you reach out to people and formally apologize for what happened, you offer them the opportunity to forgive you and feel better about what they experienced. A written apology can be a nonconfrontational way of doing just that, and hopefully it will preserve a good relationship for the future.

When constructing a written apology, it should have all of the components that I mentioned before. It should include the actual words "I'm sorry," acknowledge what harm was done, take responsibility for that harm, and explain how you will make up for it and/or why it won't happen again. Just as with a verbal apology, a written one should be done as soon as possible after you become aware that you did something wrong. You can end the letter by asking for forgiveness, because that lets the person know that what they think of you is important to you. That kind of sentiment can go a long way.

Dear Madame,

I understand that you were in the office adjacent to mine and heard me use vulgar language with my office staff. I apologize profusely for my unprofessional behavior, and I promise you that I have learned that there are better ways to address mistakes on the part of my staff and better ways of expressing myself. Since I learned of your discomfort as a result of my actions, I have endeavored to be a better person and to understand that I can still communicate effectively without profanity.

I ask that you accept my apology, and know that I will do my best moving forward to be a better physician and not fall back on this type of language.

Again, I'm so sorry that you were there to witness it. Please accept my apology, and I hope you will forgive me.

Sincerely,
Dr. Regretful

Getting the Advice of an Attorney

Just because I often advocate apologizing and taking responsibility doesn't mean I don't also advocate getting the advice of an attorney. It's important *how* you apologize, and an experienced attorney can help you find the right words. He or she can also help you see the truth about what happened and shine light on any blind spots you may have about your own behavior and your responsibility for it.

The reason I understand the components of a good apology, written or otherwise, is that people have been calling me for years, asking how to go about apologizing effectively. I've seen good apologies and not-so-good apologies. The reality is that a bad apology can do as much damage as a lie, making people feel like they're not being taken seriously and that their pain isn't being respected. That can make them even more motivated to file a complaint or seek retribution against the doctor.

As a matter of fact, if you do receive a complaint and find yourself in front of the medical board, a hot question that panelists often ask is "Well, doctor, why do you think someone would file this complaint against you?" Even if the experts have seen that your case was handled by the book and that you did everything right medically, they *still* might want to know what was at the bottom of the complaint. They still might want to know why it was filed against you instead of someone else. Sometimes it's just bad luck, but often it's about more than that.

Take the case of Dr. Fed Up, who had a bad run-in with a patient who was in poor health. Dr. Fed Up really tried to help this person, but the patient wasn't having it. The patient continued to be non-compliant with his medicine and all of the advice the doctor told him regarding his unhealthy habits that may have been contributing to the patients, illness or making it worse.

Not surprisingly, Dr. Fed Up became increasingly frustrated with this patient and she terminated the relationship and told the patient, stating that she terminated care due to his non-compliant and self-destructive behavior by going against physician advice...

A complaint came in, charging that Dr. Fed Up was guilty of unprofessional conduct, for being rude to the patient, and refusing to treat him in the future. Additionally, the doctor was charged with abandoning a patient thus putting the patient's health in danger. When the complaint ended up before the board, Dr. Fed Up's attorney counseled her to simply tell the truth and explain the full situation. The board would understand that this doctor wrote what she wrote not to be rude but because she cared about the patient and wanted him to understand what he was doing to himself. The attorney also counseled the doctor to look hard at herself. It was very understandable that she became frustrated with this patient, but might there have been a better way to express that frustration?

Dr. Fed Up could have decided, instead, to take a deep breath, let her frustration go, and say very kindly to this patient, "You need to take your medicine and revise your living habits because if you don't, you could cause serious complications. Please take me seriously this time, because you're in a dire situation, and I don't want to see that happen to you." If the doctor had said that, do you think she would have received a complaint?

Questions to Ask Yourself When Faced with a Complaint

Regardless of whether something is your fault, you should ask yourself:

- Why might someone be blaming me?
- Could my actions have contributed to this situation even if, medically, I did everything right?
- Could I have expressed more sympathy or been more caring?
- Could I have communicated better?
- Could I have been more thoughtful and responsive toward people in this situation?
- Could I have said something that would have made a difference?
- What could I have done to avoid this complaint in the first place?

Sticking It Out When the Truth Is on Your Side: Dr. Conscientious

There are occasions, although rare, where the doctor gets a complaint when he or she really has done absolutely *nothing* wrong—nothing wrong medically and nothing wrong in behavior or manner. There are cases where families were so devastated by the harm that came to their children that they blamed the doctors even though they were caring and conscientious. In such a situation, what is a doctor to do?

For this scenario, a teenage child had suffered significant head trauma from falling off a 3-Wheeler go-kart, so his parents called their primary care physician, Dr. Conscientious. At the time, the child wasn't responsive and blood was coming from his ears, so she instructed the parents to immediately bring the child to the nearest emergency room. The family did just that, and the physician, being as conscientious as she was, also contacted that ER to give the doctors there a heads-up that a patient was en route with a serious head trauma. She asked the hospital staff to make sure that Neurology was called to consult as soon as possible and that a surgical suite was prepared, just in case. Also, being familiar with the hospital because she had privileges there, she asked to speak to the doctor on call directly about the situation and give him some background on her patient.

Dr. Conscientious then proceeded to the hospital. By the time she arrived, the family was already there, and the child had been checked in for treatment. But despite her earlier calls, the ER had left the patient sitting in a room for more than thirty minutes without seeing a doctor. When Dr. Conscientious arrived and gave the name of her patient, that alerted hospital staff to check on the patient, and they finally got the ball rolling on her care.

It appeared that the hospital didn't move as fast as they should have because of a systemic breakdown in the ER. When Dr. Conscientious realized that her patient had been ignored, she proceeded to contact the neurology staff herself. Thankfully, the neurologist was in the hospital and had worked with Dr. Conscientious many times. Together they were able to see to the care of the teenager. The young patient did recover from her injuries in great thanks to the quick response by Dr. Conscientious.

Months later, a complaint was filed—not against the hospital, but against Dr. Conscientious. The complaint stated that she was not responsive to the emergency call, nonchalantly showed up at the ER very late, and was very callous in assisting in the care and treatment of the patient. It was a very sad and heartbreaking situation for this physician, because she did everything within her power to take care of the situation. What's worse, she had treated this family for many years. She never would have dreamed that they would throw these allegations at her.

Dr. Conscientious believes that, because of the heart of this family, they must have been contacted by some person on staff, who may have been responsible for ignoring the patient and family while they were waiting in the ER. To cover their mistake, the person may have encouraged the family to file this complaint against her, therefore blaming the good doctor to cover their failings. It's not always proven. In this story, Dr. Conscientious ultimately prevailed because she was able to prove—through the magic of phone records—that she'd picked up the call from the parents ASAP (not after several calls, as was alleged), and that she'd immediately contacted the hospital.

This was a case where the physician did absolutely nothing wrong. Sometimes a physician does everything right, but they just happen to be the nearest fall guy. If you've done nothing wrong medically, and there's nothing about your manner that could have been improved, then the only thing you can do is rely on the truth. That's what happened with Dr. Conscientious. Her records were impeccable, she really cared about this patient, and she had done the right things all the way through. It was a painful experience for her, but all she could do was stick it out. Eventually her blamelessness became apparent to the board, and she was rightly exonerated.

CHAPTER 7:

Correcting Chronic Bad Behavior

Any doctor can have a bad day, but the ones who are most at risk of receiving a complaint are those who have chronically bad habits. Unfortunately, when I encounter this type of physician, he or she often seems to be oblivious to the condition.

What Bad Behavior Might Look Like: Dr. Perfect-But-Unaware

Bad behavior sometimes gets hidden because other aspects of a doctor's personality overshadow it. Take the case of Dr. Perfect-But-Unaware, who was fortunate enough to be born brilliant. But because he has always been so brilliant, few have ever complained openly about him. This was true even though he was a bully growing up and everyone felt the need to stay out of his way during medical school.

His brilliance and notoriety not only led to him getting published repeatedly but also led to grateful patients donating funds to the hospital where he worked. So no one at the hospital ever complained about him either—or if they did, the complaints didn't go very far because the hospital administration protected him. This is a physician who was absolutely wonderful at his craft but who had the most horrific bedside manner.

As I discussed in an earlier chapter, not only do poor manners affect patient care, which should be your number-one priority, but they also affect morale in a hospital or office setting. I've seen this sort of situation happen multiple times: a doctor like Dr. Perfect-But-Unaware, whose bad behavior has been tolerated all through life, suddenly receives a complaint from someone who doesn't care how fancy he is. After that, his world starts to crumble.

Because Dr. Perfect-But-Unaware was indulged his whole life, he was either oblivious to his poor manners (since no one had actually called him on them) or didn't care because he believed his brilliance meant not having to worry about the niceties. That's why it came as such a shock when a complaint was filed against him by a nurse who charged that he had behaved in a rude and unprofessional manner toward her. And why it came as a further shock when his colleagues and hospital administrators didn't want to stand behind him.

When his attorney first met Dr. Perfect-But-Unaware, he was just as sweet as could be because he was suddenly in a very vulnerable position, which was new territory for him. Dr. Perfect-But-Unaware told the attorney, "I would never be rude to a nurse. It's just some kind of conspiracy to get me by someone who is jealous of what I've accomplished."

"Well, if that's the case, then justice will prevail," the attorney said. "In the meantime, we need to look at all the evidence they say they have against you." Lo and behold, what did the attorney's team find? The nurse who filed the complaint charged that when she didn't do what he asked right away (because she was busy with other things), he asked—in front of everyone—if she'd left her brain at home. That was pretty rude, but that was just the tip of the iceberg. There was twenty years' worth of internal complaints about this doctor's behavior. When a hospital decides to cooperate with the licensing agency, those deep, dark secrets tend to come out.

The hospital had never told the doctor about most of those complaints—and that ended up being part of the defense—if the doctor had been *told* he was rude, he would have apologized and changed his ways. The biggest part of preparing this doctor for his defense was getting him to realize that his behavior was indefensible. The doctor's twenty-year record was a pretty accurate reflection of him and of how others saw him. This wasn't just one little complaint but rather a clear pattern of foul language and disrespectful comments. The look on his face when his attorney pointed this out to him was like he was a little boy who'd been caught being naughty.

There were pages and pages of charges of outlandish and rude language. Some people wrote whole narratives describing the doctor's behavior and what he said, to the best of their recollection. The hospital was partially responsible for the situation because it should never have let so many complaints go without confronting him, but that's what happened, and now it was Dr. Perfect-But-Unaware who had to face the music. All he could reasonably do was admit his error, apologize for it, and work to remedy it in the future.

Diagnosing Your Own Bad Behavior

When a complaint is filed against you, it's often an opportunity to learn a lot about yourself. It gives you a chance to see yourself from someone else's perspective. Hopefully, if you suffer from chronically bad behavior, you don't have to have a complaint filed against you before you decide to do something about it. Every day is an opportunity to change, and I hope this book has already shown you some of the many reasons that it would be a good idea to do so.

If you're not sure if your behavior crosses the line—and as I mentioned before, many doctors don't see themselves for what they really are until it's too late—then you can take the following quiz to get a clearer picture of yourself. It should help you see what you're not seeing: the effect you might be having—not just on patients but on their family members, office staff, colleagues, and pretty much anyone else you encounter. If you behave poorly in your interactions with people, not only are you hurting them, but you hurt yourself in the long run because your chronically bad behavior will come home to roost.

Since many people are unable to see themselves clearly, this quiz is meant to hold up a mirror so that you can reflect upon your own behavior. Circle "yes" or "no" for each question:

Do I always strive to display professional behavior in a hospital or office setting, even when I'm not with a patient or on call?	YES NO
Do I show respect and deference to my superiors?	YES NO
Do I show respect and deference to all hospital or office staff?	YES NO
Do I show respect for my patients and pay close attention to what they say to me?	YES NO
Do I show respect for the caretakers of my patients—the people who take the time to escort them to my office or to the hospital—by acknowledging their presence and answering their questions?	YES NO

When a peer comes to me with a question about my behavior or treatment of a patient, do I listen to them with an open mind?	YES NO
Do I accept criticism and feedback easily?	YES NO
Do I accept the fact that I'm human and that I make mistakes?	YES NO
When I make a mistake or offend someone, do I openly accept responsibility?	YES NO
When I make a mistake or offend someone, am I willing to take corrective action to make up for what I've done?	YES NO
When I make a mistake, do I strive to learn from it so that I don't make the same mistake again?	YES NO
Am I quick to thank people for their help or feedback?	YES NO

Do I respond to a poor outcome by checking myself, as well as my office staff, to make sure everything was done appropriately?	YES NO
Do I seek the advice of my colleagues and ask for their review of my cases?	YES NO
Do I continue to educate myself and look for new and better ways to treat my patients?	YES NO
Finally, is my behavior similar to those around me?	YES NO
TOTAL YES	
TOTAL NO	

To score yourself, add up the number of "yes" and "no" answers that you have. If you have up to three "no" answers, you're in pretty good shape. If you have five "no" answers, you might be in the danger zone. And if you have seven "no" answers, then you could really be in trouble.

After you've tallied your score, look back at your "no" questions and think about how you could act differently in the future in each context. That last question is particularly important because it gives you a tangible way to check your behavior. Does everybody use profanity in the workplace, or are you the only one? Do others raise their voice when talking to staff? Do others keep to themselves, or do they share opinions and advice? If you find that you are very different from those around you in a particular way, you should look hard at that tendency in your behavior and ask yourself whether it's putting you at risk. You can damage your credibility, your reputation, patient care, and even your license just by behaving poorly toward the people around you. If you discover that not everybody behaves the way you do, ask yourself if you should change. Maybe you could even better yourself.

What to Do If You're a Chronic Offender

If you've examined your own behavior and think you might be a chronic offender, the question becomes: What can I do about it?

There are a number of options that are worth looking into, like courses on communication—or even anger management, if that's an issue for you. A therapist can be a great partner in helping to modify behavior. Therapy can also help relieve stress, which could be a contributing factor in your behavior.

Consulting a trusted friend or colleague is another great option, especially if you want an honest opinion on your manners from someone who sees you in action. There are also mentoring programs available to physicians at different medical societies throughout the country. They will pair you with a fellow physician whom you can consult on a regular basis—by phone or in person—about different approaches and situations. Listening to how someone else might have handled or thought through an issue that you've encountered can be very enlightening. This is an easy thing for any physician to do, as it doesn't take a lot of time or paperwork. Even if you think you have the perfect manners for a doctor, a mentor can be a great way to check on yourself regularly, let off steam, get another take on something, or just talk through how you can continue to be the best doctor you can be.

Whether it's informally with a friend or a colleague, or you opt for something more formal like a mentoring program, that kind of camaraderie is important. Seeing situations—or *yourself*—through someone else's eyes can help you keep your perspective. And that's important because you don't become one of those physicians who is genuinely shocked to find out that his or her file at the hospital contains pages and pages of complaints about bad behavior.

Another thing that is incredibly important to do—for all doctors, not just chronic offenders—is to take some time on a regular basis to simply reflect on your day. Sometimes doctors get so caught up in what they have to do that they don't get a chance to think about how they're handling things and how they might do better in the future. You can accomplish this by keeping a log or journal where you record the events of the day or by simply taking some time to personally reflect on how things went in terms of patient care, interactions between hospital or office staff, and procedures that were or weren't followed. This will help you catch problems before they turn into bad habits, as well as help you become accountable to yourself.

In summary, if its determined that you need to improve your behavior, you may wish to consider:

- taking courses in subjects like communication or anger management
- seeing a therapist to help with behavior modification
- asking a friend or colleague to consult with you or be an accountability partner
- doing this in a more formal way through a peer mentoring program
- keeping a journal of what happened during the day and how you reacted
- taking time to reflect on your actions and behaviors

There's Always Hope: Dr. Without-a-Clue

Dr. Without-a-Clue received a complaint where it was alleged that he displayed unprofessional conduct with hospital staff. "I don't understand what this allegation is about," he said when he first called. "It says I was unprofessional with hospital staff, but that's ridiculous. I've been a physician for more than twenty-five years, and I am the epitome of professionalism. My medical record's always superb. I'm never late. I always respond to my pages and my calls when I am on call. And I give my patients the best possible care."

Once the evidence packet came in from the reviewing entity, the attorney was able to see specific evidence tied to the allegations. In preparation for the scheduled hearing to review this case, the attorney called the doctor into her office to discuss the details of the case and the evidence packet. Starting with the specific allegations, the attorney said, "Doctor, the allegations said you use vulgar language when speaking to hospital staff. Is that true? Is that something you do?"

"I have absolutely no idea what they're talking about," he replied, and he wasn't lying. Dr. Without-a-Clue genuinely did not know that his language was foul, even though it clearly was by any reasonable standard. That was because Dr. Without-a-Clue had been brought up in an environment where speaking coarsely was commonplace and part of the culture. It was also acceptable in the place where he did his residency. So no one had ever called him on it because most of the people around him spoke the same way.

The doctor expected the complaint to be resolved quickly because he was that sure he hadn't done anything wrong. However, it was not resolved quickly. In fact, the reviewing agency announced that there would be a hearing on the complaint, which of course astounded the doctor. When a hearing is scheduled to take place, the board will send you a packet of evidence so that you can prepare. And in the packet of evidence were even more details. In fact, it included more than a dozen reports from nurses and other staff going back twenty-five years, claiming this physician had been offensive, vulgar, and all sorts of other unsavory things.

The meeting lasted about two hours. Finally, Dr. Without-a-Clue threw his hands up. He was out of excuses.

"Doctor, with all due respect, I'm not a psychologist, but I think this is what's called denial," the attorney said. "You've been giving me a smoke screen. I could understand if it were just one bad report—that we could question— but more than a dozen reports with detailed descriptions of what took place is something else. I think we have a real problem here."

Eventually, Dr. Without-a-Clue stopped giving excuses and admitted that he had said things that could be considered inappropriate. Later, he even admitted that his language was offensive.

Before appearing before the board, his attorney suggested a proactive approach and helped the doctor prepare a letter of apology to those he had offended. He also enrolled in a communication course. The good news was that he was not as a rule a mean-spirited person, but his language was pretty terrible—even to the point where it could have affected patient care because so many nurses and other staff members were walking on eggshells around him and trying to avoid being in his presence. That is a real red flag for a medical board. If staff members are so distraught or distracted that it could get in the way of their care of the patient, then the medical board is going to take that very seriously.

So this doctor, after twenty-five years, rectified his behavior. Not only did he take the course and write the apologies, but he got in the habit only saying things to his patients and peers that he would be comfortable saying to his priest, his rabbi, or his grandmother. It became the rule. When he got in front of the medical board, he didn't put up a defense. Instead, he acknowledged responsibility and talked to them about what he was doing to make things right. The board accepted his acts of contrition, and he really did change his behavior over the long term.

It was really the best possible outcome to a difficult situation. If the doctor hadn't admitted to his mistakes, how could the board have believed he would never commit them again? They couldn't have, and he probably would have continued on as before. But by saying he was sorry—specifically acknowledging what he was sorry for—and then implementing a plan for making things right in the future, he was not only able to change his behavior, but he also gave others the opportunity to trust and believe in him going forward.

CHAPTER 8:

Advice for Retiring Physicians

This chapter is about doctors who are nearing the end of their career and may be facing some different considerations than doctors at the height of their career. That said, I hope that all doctors will read it. It's a good idea for doctors of any age to be aware of what they could be facing when eventually they near retirement so that they can prepare for the future. Retirement-age doctors who have made it through their entire career without a complaint are probably not in danger of making the kinds of errors in manners that some of their younger colleagues might commit. But with age comes not only great experience and great knowledge but also a different set of potential issues to consider.

With age can come things like health issues, cognitive issues, and issues where someone is stuck in a rut, treating patients the same way he or she always has rather than keeping up with the latest research, procedures, and technologies. The question of when to retire is a tricky one, and it's one that sometimes physicians and those around them may disagree on, which can cause a lot of tension.

Health Issues

When it comes to health issues, I've seen many, many situations where doctors are forced to take into account the fact that their bodies don't work as well as they used to, and that's not an easy thing to admit. For example, take the very common problem of diminished eyesight as you age. If you're a psychiatrist, then your ability to see does not necessarily impair your ability to practice medicine because your job is more about listening to what your patient has to say. You may have to make some adjustments in the way you work, like in the way you keep notes on patients, but because we live in the age of technology, you could, for example, dictate your notes instead of writing them down. It could be argued that you can still practice very effectively despite changes in your eyesight.

However, if you're a surgeon, failing eyesight can be a much bigger problem. It could even lead to the medical board revoking your license. It is not always easy to know when you have crossed the line between your eyes just not being what they used to be and your eyes being bad enough to impair your abilities as a surgeon.

When they *do* cross over that line, many physicians who have enjoyed many years of practice and to whom the practice of medicine is, in fact, their life, have a hard time accepting it. Some even go into denial. I've seen doctors who say, "I don't have any problems with my hand-eye coordination," even though they can barely hold the pen to sign the contract that allows me to represent them. I've had others tell me they are in perfect health, despite the fact that their children called ahead of time to let me know they'd been diagnosed with terminal cancer.

Of course, not all health problems mean your time practicing medicine has to come to an end—but when health does become an issue, I really feel for the physicians. Dealing with the loss of one's health and the loss of one's career—a career that may well have been a big part of your very identity—is extremely difficult. That's when I have to sit across the table from a physician and say, "Doctor, you have had a long, wonderful career. I want you to seriously consider retiring with dignity and using your talents in other ways—maybe to mentor younger doctors, lecture on your area of expertise, write your memoirs, or do something for yourself after a lifetime of taking care of others."

That phrase "retiring with dignity" is something I believe all physicians should consider, hopefully well before they need to. Ask yourself what retiring with dignity would mean to you, and prepare for that—so that when the day eventually comes, it's less of a hardship. Also, think about things you *don't* want to happen at the end of your illustrious career. One of the most heartbreaking things I've seen in my career has been when doctors who have had long and honorable careers get their licenses taken from them by the medical board against their will. If it is brought to the board's attention that your health is compromised in a way that might affect patient care, then they absolutely can request or even require an evaluation from a forensic physician in your specialty, which could lead to the loss of your license.

In such cases, I get a team of people in place to assist the doctor in considering this moment in his or her life. Generally, the team consists of me and members of their family, such as the spouse and/or children, and sometimes a friend or colleague. We have to be very honest, but gentle, about helping the doctor see what his or her limitations are. Maybe he or she is forgetting appointments or has an unsteady hand or is just too ill to keep up the schedule like before. And then we talk about the benefits of voluntarily giving up his or her license.

It's a personal decision, of course, but I think it's much better all-around if a doctor can face the realities and make that decision for him or herself, rather than having to do so because of a complaint or pressure from the medical board.

These are good questions for doctors of any age to be asking themselves, but particularly those nearing retirement:

- What would retiring with dignity look like for me personally?
- What do I *not* want to happen at the end of my career? How can I avoid that?
- How will I continue to contribute to society and live my life to the fullest after I stop practicing medicine?

Ageism: Dr. Elder

The elephant in the room when complaints arise against doctors nearing retirement age is prejudice against age. This kind of prejudice definitely exists in the medical field.

At the end of the day, if you're an older physician who finds yourself on the receiving end of a complaint, the question of your age, whether it's specifically laid out in the allegations or not, is likely to become an issue, even if your case is otherwise absolutely dismissable.

Let's say Dr. Elder, an established doctor who has been the only doctor in his small town for many years, started hearing about a young upstart doctor who recently came to town to open a practice. All the people in the town have been saying under their breath that this young doctor is essentially going to become Dr. Elder's replacement, but Dr. Elder doesn't see it that way. Then a complaint comes in from this new physician. She has treated an established patient of Dr. Elder and saw that Dr. Elder diagnosed a patient with rheumatism when the patient actually had terminal cancer. The cancer had now progressed to a point where nothing could be done to save the patient, so the complaint was for failure to diagnose.

These are dire possibilities that could come from Dr. Elder's knowledge being outdated or from him being stuck in his ways. But it could also happen for other reasons. Dr. Elder could actually be a brilliant physician who has known this patient her whole life. He might, in fact, have discovered his patient's cancer and known it was terminal, but rather than tell her and reduce her quality of life for the short time she had left, he chose to keep that information to himself and simply treat her pain. Of course, as soon as a complaint like that comes in, the board will be looking at Dr. Elder, and rightly or wrongly, they are almost surely going to wonder if his age was a contributing factor. Is he still on his game? Is he up to date on the latest procedures, tests, and medications? All this could come up simply because some new doctor who wants to establish a competing practice files a complaint without full knowledge of the situation.

It may not be fair, but unfortunately, ageism is real. So the question that physicians should ask themselves is: Do I want to consider retiring with dignity after practicing for fifty years, or do I want to risk getting a complaint and having to defend my abilities amid questions about my age? You can't control the actions of human beings, and you could get a complaint that is clearly viable—but because of the fact that you happen to be senior, your age will be considered.

It's possible, in cases where a complaint isn't viable, that the board will look at an aging physician and say, "In lieu of disciplining you for this violation of board rules and regulations, we would like to offer you a voluntary surrender of license." That may be very upsetting for the doctor, who may consider it to be discrimination. In this country, we don't like the idea of that kind of prejudice, and it can certainly be fought. However, it is still a fact of life that many aging physicians will have to face. And whether or not it's worth fighting to have a few more years of practice is a question I've seen many doctors struggle with.

There is no right or easy answer to this, and doctors have to decide for themselves. Hopefully, they are capable of judging their own situation and abilities realistically, and if they can, my response is always, "Doctor, you should practice for as long as you feel strong enough and healthy enough to do it, but I still want you to be aware of the danger because once you reach a certain age, there may be a kind a target on your head because of how old you are. At some point, even if it's unfair, you may need to ask yourself whether it's worth the fight."

If a doctor *does* want to fight a complaint, my advice is always to be proactive. Assume that your age is likely to be an issue, either overtly or in the back of the board's mind, and take steps to show them that it's a nonissue before they ask about it. I ask the doctor to get a report in writing from his or her personal physician showing what good health he or she is in, and I include that in the evidence packet, even though it hasn't been asked for. I make it clear that even if the doctor is in his seventies, for example, he still runs marathons or whatever the particular situation may be. I want to anticipate and thwart any concerns the board might have.

Being Prepared for Retirement

Because I've seen so many doctors struggle with the decision of when to retire, I counsel doctors of any age to be prepared. It's a decision that they will have to make at one time or another, and it's much better to make it on their own terms than because of a complaint or because of pressure from those who care about them.

One of the best ways doctors can prepare themselves is to live a well-rounded life. That means developing hobbies, interests, a strong family life, and not letting medicine be the only thing in their lives. It's the doctors for whom their practice is their whole life and identity who struggle the most with retirement. And that can lead them to make some bad decisions—like continuing to practice when they are really too ill to do so.

It's important to remember that medicine is what you *do*, not who you *are*. If you were in a car accident tomorrow and could no longer practice, that wouldn't make anything you've achieved in your life less meaningful, nor would it mean that you wouldn't still have a lot to offer. The same should be said of a physician at the end of a career. I certainly understand that great focus and determination is necessary to be the best at what you do. But focusing on one thing at the expense of a full, well-rounded life can also lead to some of the behavioral issues that we've talked about throughout this book. It is physicians like that—who don't know how to relieve their stress, who don't take the time to develop relationships, and who don't think things like communication and a good working environment are that important—who end up getting into trouble.

Spending time with your family, traveling the world, developing outside interests in anything from sports to cooking, or just appreciating the simple things in life—these are things that will give you zest for life in *addition* to practicing amazing medicine. These are things that will make your life feel full even after you've retired. And you can start developing these things at any age, the earlier the better. I have a demanding career, too, so I understand the barriers, but as my husband always says to me, "Honey, it's not about having the time to do things; it's about *making* the time to do them."

Continuing to Use Your Talents

When I have to sit across from doctors and talk to them about giving up their licenses, one of the things that is crucially important to think about is how they can continue to give back to the world because someone with that much training and experience certainly has a lot to give. It just might have to be given in a different way. For many physicians, ceasing to practice may not really be retirement at all. It's about laying down one mantle and picking up another.

That physician may have been in a position to really understand where more medical research or better facilities are needed in his or her community or specialty. I've seen physicians go on to become philanthropists and advocates for truly important causes. I talked earlier in this book about mentorship and how that can be a very valuable tool for physicians who need to work on some aspect of themselves or their profession. A doctor who is no longer practicing can act as a great mentor to someone in that position, really helping him or her through and shaping his or her career. Teaching or lecturing are also great ways for someone to put knowledge and years of experience to further use.

I've also known doctors to go on to have full second careers. Some have pursued research in the lab rather than treating patients. Some have gone on to have political careers and helped draft laws that make medicine better. Retirement shouldn't be a dirty word; it should simply be an opportunity to reshape your life in a new way.

A Final Word

I hope this book has given physicians and others in the medical field plenty to think about with regard to the manner in which they practice medicine. If there are only two points you take away from this book, I believe it should be these:

1. *Be a human being first and a doctor second.* This means that your ability to diagnose illnesses and your ability to wield a scalpel are just one part of a broader skill set that you continue to develop with compassion, humility, kindness, respect, and good communication. Hopefully, this book has shown how vitally important that really is.

2. *There is a lesson in every experience.* This is true even in a complaint, and even in a complaint that ends badly. Every experience is an opportunity to learn more about yourself and find ways to be better at what you do and be a better person overall.

Dr. Goodfellow, for example, was preparing for a very difficult hearing. When good attorneys work with doctors who have been on the receiving end of a complaint, one of the things we often need to do in order to prove that they're competent and professional is to get recommendations attesting to their good character and habits. When I first ask clients what someone might say about them in such a letter, they often say, "You know, I really don't know."

Then they will go ahead and ask people they know for recommendation letters; anyone will tell you how great it feels when they read and hear wonderful things about themselves, even the most humble of people. That's exactly what happened in the story of Dr. Goodfellow.

The letters supporting Dr. Goodfellow started pouring in. It was like that old Christmas movie, *Miracle on 34th Street*, where an attorney was trying to prove that Santa Claus was, in fact, Santa Claus. And so he walks into the courtroom and pours all these letters on top of the judge's bench from children who had written to Santa Claus (*Miracle on 34th Street*, directed by George Seaton, Twentieth Century Fox Film Corporation, 1947).

The letters said things like, "I've known Dr. Goodfellow for twenty years. We met in medical school, and he impressed me from the very start. He's one of those guys whose smile is infectious, and he is a joy to work with. I've often heard patients talk about what a wonderful doctor he is and how he actually takes the time to listen to them. Because of that, when I have a patient who's in need of his specialty, I refer them to him. Those patients always come back with good reports about what a great doctor he is, and what a great guy he is." There were also letters from patients, saying, "This doctor not only saved my life, but he made me feel like I could make it through my illness every step of the way. I am better off not only because he cured me but because I got a chance to know what a wonderful person he is inside."

Dr. Goodfellow got really choked up when he heard what people were saying about him—who wouldn't want to be spoken about like that? It was a testament to his good work and to the good person that he was for practicing medicine with such care and respect for his fellow human beings.

It's in situations like this that I lean in toward these doctors and remind them what their true purpose in life is and how noble that purpose really is. I would have said to Dr. Goodfellow, "Doctor, I want you to remember who you are. You are not the sum of what's written on this complaint. You are a good person and a good physician. I want you to remember why you went into medicine, which was to help people and to heal people. I want you to remember how much you have given to so many people over the years. I want you to think about how much you still have to give to the people in this great state. That's who you are—not what's written about you in this allegation."

When facing these horrible moments in life, when someone is questioning your actions or even considering whether or not you should continue to practice medicine at all, what's most important is to know in your heart of hearts that you have done the best that you could and that you will continue to do your best no matter how things turn out. That's a difficult thing to remember when you're afraid of what's going to happen to the career you've worked so hard for. But it's also in moments like these that people learn something about who they really are. They are reminded of what is most important. In this way, even the most difficult circumstance can be an enlightening and educational experience in the long run.

If this is the situation you find yourself in, no matter what you did or didn't do, the first lesson you can draw from your current experience is that you are a human being.

You are capable of error. If you have made an error, the best thing you can do is proceed in truth and do your best to make up for it and ensure that it will never happen again.

Another lesson is that no matter what flaws you have or what mistakes you may have made, you decided to use the gift that God gave you to heal others—and that puts you in a whole other stratosphere of grace and beauty in my eyes. We look to our doctors as our saviors in this world. We look to them to help us when we're at our worst. We look to them for security, for comfort, for hope. You may not have always lived up to that ideal in the past, but you can always strive to live up to it now and in the future.

I truly believe these are crucial lessons to keep in mind because what your patients need at the end of the day is a healthy doctor, a focused doctor, a happier doctor— someone who is not walking into the office with a chip on their shoulder or overly exhausted. We all want a doctor who practices medicine with joy, with dignity, and with the purpose of serving others. Because at the end of the day, all doctors should be servants to their craft and servants to their patients. To be a great leader is to first be a great servant, and my model for that is where my deepest, most personal belief lies. For the most part, this has been a secular book, but I am not a secular author. I am an author of great faith—and so my hero when it comes to the best leader there ever was is my Lord. And to me, "it is written."

I believe that everyone who gets into the field of medicine does so because they want to help others, to be of service, to make a difference in people's lives. All human beings are capable of making a positive difference in the lives of others, though sometimes some of us forget our purpose along the road of life. Sometimes doctors forget what drew them to medicine in the first place. They get distracted by the needs of the everyday—the need to make money, the need to please their fellow physicians or superiors, and the need to juggle the various forces that pressure them in one way or another. Sometimes like any man or woman, physicians may need a negative event in their lives to remind them that their true purpose as the healthcare provider is to make that positive difference in the lives of their patients, each and every day. And what could be more noble than that?

God did not bless me with the ability to heal, but he blessed me with the honor of protecting those that do. I consider that a great responsibility. I've become the biggest fan of the doctors that I have had the pleasure to work with as clients, as well as experts in the field of medicine. When people ask my son, "What does your mom do for a living?" my awesome fourth-grader says, "My mom protects doctors for a living."

I love the sweet and simple way my young child puts it. He thinks of me as Supermom protecting doctors for the world. And that's the ideal that I strive to live up to every day. It is the desire to protect the doctors that inspired me to write these fictitious scenarios or parables to give snapshots of just some of the events that could happen. Use these stories to enhance your practice, if you will, to share with colleagues, friends, and students of medicine.

To our brave and noble doctors, leading the fight against death and disease, thank you for being heroes and champions in the world of your patients and for the families of your patients. You are appreciated. Hold on to your purpose with courage and grace. May the stories in this book, written in honor of you, entertain, enlighten and enhance the gift of good old-fashioned manners I know you possess.

How Can We Help?

Law Office of Victoria Soto

www.vsotomedlaw.com

401 Congress Avenue #1540

Austin, TX 78701

Phone: 512-852-3055

Fax: 512-687-6202

1 Chisholm Trail, Suite 150

Round Rock, TX 78681

Phone: 512-341-9600

Fax: 512-341-9688

Victoria Soto, JD, and her team at the Law Office of Victoria Soto offer a variety of services in law as well as speaking and consulting to help today's health-care professionals improve their talents and skills to become even greater leaders in their fields. For more information, visit www.vsotomedlaw.com.

Health Law Defense Attorney

The Law Office of Victoria Soto is focused on defending healthcare professionals before their licensing agencies. Victoria and her team also advise these professionals as they seek licensure and provide mediation in workplace disputes.

Speaking and Consulting

As a keynote and motivational speaker, Victoria regularly lectures at business/law and health conferences on leadership, risk management, and human relations.

She also offers a thought-provoking course, "World's Best Doctors," at group and corporate retreats to show doctors easy, effective ways to incorporate good behavioral patterns to build even more successful careers in medicine.

Printed in the USA
CPSIA information can be obtained
at www.ICGtesting.com
JSHW012031140824
68134JS00033B/2992

9 781599 326320